THE STOKESHIRE

THE STORY OF PEMBROKESHIRE

WENDY HUGHES

Gwasg Carreg Gwalch

ISBN: 0-86381-253-8

Map: Ken Lloyd Gruffydd

First published in 1993 by Gwasg Carreg Gwalch,

Printed in Wales

Dedication

For my sons, Richard and Craig with love.

Also by the same author:
THE STORY OF GOWER

Contents

Author's Note

This book could not have been written without reference to the many authors who have researched Pembrokeshire before me, and a selected list appears at the end of this book. Also thanks to the people, too numerous to mention, who made us welcome and were only too willing to share stories with us on our stays in the area.

I would like to express my thanks to the following people whose assistance and help turned writing this book into an enjoyable task.

Conrad Hughes, who again tramped the muddy lanes and clambered down the cliffs in order to produce the majority of the photographs.

The Welsh Folk Museum for their help and permission to use some of their photographs.

Cass and Janie Jackson for all their expert advice and proof reading.

All my friends at London Writers Circle and Elmbridge Writers who have always been on hand to offer constructive criticism and sound advice.

Myrddin ap Dafydd for whom it has been a pleasure to work.

Introduction

Pembrokeshire is known as the land of cromlechs and castles, but to past generations it was *Gwlad Hud a Lledrith* — the land of mystery and enchantment. It is the home of two branches of the *Mabinogi*, those four classic stories concerning Pwyll Prince of Dyfed, Branwen daughter of Llŷr, Manawydan son of Llŷr, and Math son of Mathonwy, which together with other Welsh myths and legends, give the reader a clear glimpse into the murky mists of the early Celtic period.

Off the coast of Pembrokeshire lay the lush green islands of enchantment, where the *plant Rhys Ddwyn* — children of Rees the Deep — lived. This is the name the West Wales people give to the *Tylwyth Teg*, the Fair Folk, or the Welsh fairies, who used to frequent the markets of Haverfordwest, Milford and Fishguard until the 19th century. They were only seen by a few sharp-eyed folk and those who were blessed with the gift of second sight. Without speaking these little people, who varied from the size of a thumb to the size of a young child, would buy their meat, corn and household goods, placing silver pennies on the counter as if knowing what they would be charged. The local farmers liked them because they bought well, often paying 'over the odds' for goods, but the poorer people detested them because they forced the price of goods up.

Pembrokeshire possesses everything, including breathtaking scenery, unique rock formations and natural blow holes which are at their most spectacular during stormy weather. Here you will see a wealth of fascinating archaeological monuments, and learn the mystery of the Preseli Bluestones. Also a geological history that is one of the oldest in the world giving us a glimpse of what lived in the sea millions of years ago.

It also has a profusion of wildlife ranging from the Atlantic grey seal, to the guillemots, dolphins and porpoises. The fox and the badger too are common, with the polecat and the mink frequently sighted. There is also an abundance of rare and wild flowers. The moorland is thickly carpeted with heather and western gorse, whilst the cliffs sport red and white campion, and bird's foot trefoil in the spring. There are two types of rock-sea lavender which can only be found in Ireland and Pembrokeshire.

A day-time tripper to Skomer in February would be unaware that beneath his feet is the largest concentration in the world of manx shearwaters, over 100,000 pairs, who have arrived from South America to establish their breeding sites.

Pembrokeshire, known as the 'premier' county of Wales, existed for eight and half centuries until local government reorganisation in 1974. Now, sadly, it has been amalgamated with Cardigan and Carmarthen to form Dyfed, although there is talk of it reverting to the old county names. However, to the folk of Pembrokeshire, it has always been their county, and the name survives in the names of institutions like Pembrokeshire Cricket Club and Pembrokeshire Agricultural Society, not forgetting the Pembrokeshire corgis.

Henry Tudor was born at Pembroke castle, and returned from exile in France in 1485, landing at Dale to defeat Richard III at Bosworth field. From that day the Tudor dynasty was formed and this is not forgotten either, with the Tudor Rose forming the centre piece of the official Pembrokeshire flag.

Anyone visiting Pembrokeshire can be certain of a warm welcome in more ways than one. Far to the West of Wales it is warmed by the Gulf Stream, making the weather so mild, that over 50 species of flowers have been recorded in bloom as early as January.

Food is a speciality of Pembrokeshire, with Pembrokeshire potatoes, Pembrokeshire turkey, Welsh lamb and home grown vegetables high on the menu. The Welsh name, Penfro from which Pembroke derives, means 'the end of the land' and with Pembrokeshire surrounded on three sides by the sea the fruits of the sea are not to be forgotten either. If you want to be adventurous I recommend laverbread, a delicacy made from seaweed, which accompanied with bacon makes a delicious Welshman's breakfast. But be warned it is an acquired taste, and leaves many a puzzled visitor staring at the 'Welsh caviare' in disbelief.

There are an assortment of information centres in Pembrokeshire to help visitors make the most of their stay. A wide range of changing and permanent exhibitions, over 300 walks with guides who are only too willing to point out places of interest and tell you a little of the history.

For the less energetic there are the bus tours and the boat trips around the coast or to Caldy Island. For the more active there are hills to climb, remote villages to visit, and sailing dinghies to hire. But whatever your fitness no visit will be complete without even a short walk along the Pembrokeshire Coastal Path. Before we admire the scenery let's sit back and take a glimpse into Pembrokeshire's ancient past.

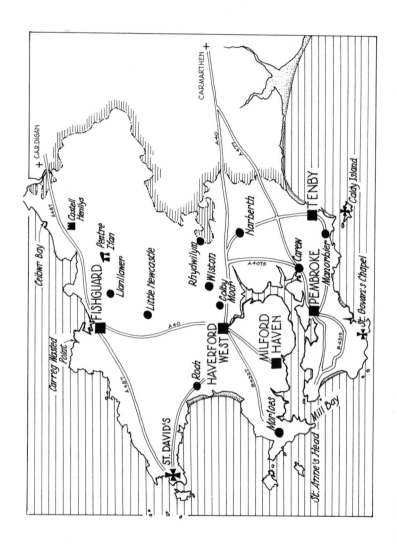

CHAPTER ONE

The Early Settlers

The area covered in this book, the old county of Pembrokeshire, began over a thousand million years ago when a series of explosive volcanoes erupted. The flowing molten liquid, from within the earth's crust, cooled and solidified to form igneous rocks. The most ancient of these, the Pre-Cambrian rocks, can be found on St David's peninsula, that wild rugged coastline from Stumble Head to Ramsey Island, and also at Trefgarn, Johnston, Talbenni, Benton and Roch. The sediment that settled at the bottom of the liquid has revealed many interesting fossilised items, including water fleas and brachiopods, or 'lamp-shells', because they resemble a Roman oil lamp, telling us about the life that once lay beneath the Pembrokeshire sea some 500 million years ago. The most interesting of these, an enormous trilobite, a woodlouse like crustacean, nearly two feet in length was found accidentally by John William Salter in 1862 at Porth-y-rhaw, near St David's. In a paper, presented to Fellows of the Geological Society of London in February 1863, he stated 'My object now is to point out the locality and geological place of a giant Trilobite long looked for in Britain, and lately, I must say accidentally, found by me. I believed I was working at Solva Harbour, in Llandeilo Flags, but by good fortune I had landed instead in a parallel creek a mile or so westward, at the junction of the red and purple Cambrian grits with the Lingula-slates . . . The fry of some large Trilobite first attracted my attention, and then by looking along the ledges, I found fragments (head, body-rings, labrum), but none perfect, of the largest species of Paradoxides known, scarcely excepting the great P. Harlani from near

Boston. Agnostus accompanied it, as usual, being the smallest as Paradoxides is the largest, Trilobite of the primordial zone.'

As you can imagine, Salter's discovery caused excitement and brought a steady stream of geologists and collectors to Porth-y-rhaw, with the result that it is now difficult to find more than small fragments of these crustaceans.

To the north of the county we find the Ordovician and Silurian rocks which once formed the sea bed. When further volcanic activities occurred they erupted such that the Ordovician rocks now form the headland of Penmaendewi and Penclegyr, and stretch the full length of the Preseli Hills. The Silurian rocks can be seen from St Dogmael's to Newport sands, from Narberth to Haverfordwest, from Freshwater East to Freshwater West, and from St Ishmael's to Skomer. About 400 million years ago, as this particular period came to an end, the Caledonian mountain chain wrinkled and creased into folds, giving us some spectacular cliff faces at Pen-yr-afr and Ceibwr today.

Rims of red sandstone, limestone and carboniferous rocks formed another geographical area that can be found in south Pembrokeshire. This contained much of the famous Pembroke anthracite coal, valued by the early industrialists because of its heating and low ash qualities.

At the end of this period another movement known as the Armorican orogeny, because it's nucleus was in Armorica — now Brittany — pushed Pembrokeshire further up against the north. The three tall cliffs, known as the three chimneys, that stand on end at Marloes Sands are a consequence of this.

The sea has drowned the land on several occasions. Two million years ago the sea was 600 feet above its present level, and reached the base of the Preseli mountains, leaving a plateau that still survives to the north east of Newport and around Maenclochog today. Later the sea level dropped 200 ft and formed a surface between Dinas and Fishguard, and around Mathri and Croesgoch. Later it fell a further 200 feet to form the level platform that covers much of the coast land of south Pembrokeshire today.

The evidence of ice-scratch rock surfaces on Carn Ingli, and the existence of widespread boulder clay suggests that about a 100 thousand years ago, Pembrokeshire was completely submerged in glacier ice. As the ice covering the area began to melt, it isolated Carn Ingli from the Preseli

14

Pentre Ifan Cromlech

The creased and wrinkled rocks at Ceibwr Bay

Hills. Finally when the ice melted, the sea rose again and drowned the valleys of Nevern, the Solfach, and a large number of ancient forests became submerged. Today, at low tide, these forests are exposed at Whitesand Bay, Lydstep, Newport, Amroth and Saundersfoot.

The earliest known human occupation of Pembrokeshire occurred during the later cold stages of the Ice Age when it was winter all the year round. One of the earliest species of man as we know him today, Neanderthalers or hunters, sought shelter in the limestone caves on Caldy Island, around Tenby, Cathole Quarry, and on the Pembroke river banks. He had a heavy jaw and receding chin and walked less upright than modern man. However, he was intelligent enough to know how to hunt and how to dress the skins of the animals he killed. He lit fires in the cave entrances as a protection against the biting cold climate and to warn off any wild animals. The population of Neanderthal man was sparse in Wales and we can only assume that as flint, primitive man's best raw material, was a rare commodity in Wales, this explains his limited presence.

Around 22 thousand years ago a new race, the Old Stone Age, or Palaeolithic man, related to the Co-Magnon race who so cleverly painted the caves in Southern France, arrived in Wales.

12 thousand years later, at the end of the last Ice Age, the sea-level around the coast of Wales rose once more. The water from melting ice caps rushed into the sea and carved out the Gwaun Valley where today the River Gwaun meanders gently down to meet the sea at Fishguard. It was also during this period that many of the fascinating legends of drowned kingdoms around the coast of Wales came into existence.

About this time also the Old Stone Age settlements were being replaced by the Mesolithic, or Middle Stone Age people. These inhabitants, especially those who occupied Nanna's Cave on Caldy Island, had learnt new skills of stone chipping and produced small neatly trimmed blades. With the discovery of a number of animal bones we are reminded that Caldy Island was once a hill surrounded by a wooded plain that now lies deep beneath the sea.

Until 1960 it was assumed that these settlers lived on the coast within easy reach of the sea, but a discovery of a hoard of flints high in the Glamorganshire mountains suggests that these folk had become adventuresome, moving in search of their prey. Evidence indicates that after 5000 BC the climate of Wales was very similar to today, with densely wooded forests extending into green valleys.

Around 5 thousand years ago, with Britain now cut off from France, the next people to arrive in Pembrokeshire were the Neolithic farmers. They arrived by sea, probably sailing up the Bristol Channel in a simple animal skin and wattle vessel, similar to the Welsh coracle that can be seen on the rivers of Wales today. The reason these vessels have continued to be useful is because they are light and portable and can be carried easily by one man on his back, giving him the appearance of an overgrown beetle. These farmers usually settled within sight of the sea and began to build themselves huts. They would have been built between two steps of rock with a wooden roof which was supported on eight timber posts. At Clegyr Boia, near St David's cathedral, archaeologists have been able to make a reconstruction of such a hut. There is evidence of other buildings on the hill, suggesting that this could have been the first farming community in Wales.

The Neolithic folk were a dark haired race with a distinctive long head. They raised cattle and sheep and supplemented their diet by hunting, gathering fruit, roots and nuts. They weaved cloth from the wool of their sheep, made rope from hair and were a community of potters. They also made wooden handles for their flint weapons but knew nothing about metals.

But they are best remembered by their chambered tombs or cromlechau — shelter stones, which comprised of a large capstone resting on stone pillars and covered with a mound of earth or stone. Over thirty of these historic relics are still visible, mostly in north Pembrokeshire, littering the Preseli mountains. It is not surprising to learn that, because of their sheer size, these monuments have been linked with many legends of heroes and giants. They were once regarded as the graves of giants, blacksmiths anvils and the 'quoits' (a game where an object is tossed at a stake) of King Arthur, the devil and Samson.

In north Pembrokeshire there is a mysterious series of Samson monuments, among the best known being Carreg Samson, at Longhouse above Abercastle. According to legend, Samson raised this with his little finger which he then lost and buried in Bedd Bys Samson, the grave of

Samson's finger, on Ynys y Castell, an inlet that could have been an early Christian site. At Nevern there is another Bedd Samson — Samson's grave — and near Nicholas, Ffyst Samson — Samson's flail, an implement for threshing grain. Why they are named after Samson is one of Pembrokeshire's many curiosities, although some say they were named later after the 6th century abbot of Caldy Island and Dol in Brittany. He was one of the best known of Brittany's Seven Thousand, Seven Hundred, Seven Score and Seven Saints, and is the patron saint of Brittany today.

Stackpole Warren has been established, by the Dyfed Archaeological Trust, as the site of a prehistoric village. Beneath a standing stone, known as the Devil's Quoit, were found the burnt remains of a wooden hut with cremated human remains in the middle of the floor. A bronze harp shaped brooch was also discovered. Legend states the Devil's Quoit and two nearby stones come together at Saxon's Ford on Midsummer Eve to dance before resuming their places.

The most spectacular among these cromlechau is the Pentre Ifan Cromlech which was one of the first burial chambers to be conserved under the Ancient Monuments Act, and has a mystical air about it. The huge capstone is about 17ft by 10ft and tips back from its cover, resting on a single pointed upright at the back, giving it a 'floating' effect. The site was first excavated in 1936-37 and it has been suggested that the original barrow was possibly over 150ft long, 65ft wide and at least 11ft high. It was excavated again in 1958-9, and the central tomb was found to lie in an oval pit. Finds from these excavations were disappointing, but they did include some Neolithic pottery and a few flint tools. Historians now suggest several phases of building are represented at Pentre Ifan. Every Pembrokeshire maiden will tell you that if she crawled around a cromlech three times at full moon, she would see, in the moonlight, a vision of the man she would marry. If a young man fell asleep under the giant capstones he would either go mad or become a great poet. Is this the reason why there have been so many talented Welsh poets I wonder?

The most puzzling prehistoric monuments in Pembrokeshire are the Menhir, or Standing Stones. That great Welsh historian, Giraldus Cambrensis, Gerald of Wales, believed that they were erected to mark the victories of King Harold over the Welsh in 1063. There is no evidence to

Parcymeirw at Llanllawer

Gors Fawr Circle

support his claim and some believe they may have been monuments or cult objects associated with fertility and date to the Bronze Age. They sometimes appear in pairs, one taller and more tapering than the other — male and female like the ancient stones at Avebury. Excavations at the Rhosyclegyrn stone, near St Nicholas, revealed evidence of ritual practices.

An alignment of eight stones at Parcymeirw, *Field of the Dead*, near Llanychâr, is one of only eight in Wales and one of the most amazing relics left by our ancestors. The stones range from five to twelve feet in height and span a total distance of some 40 metres. Their purpose remains a mystery, although modern research proves that it was used as a lunar observatory by megalithic inhabitants for predicting eclipses. It uses a visible mountain in the Wicklow Hills in Ireland, some 91 miles away, as one end of a long sight line, and works only when the moon appears to set by sliding down the right hand side of Mount Leinster indicating that an eclipse is imminent. It is so simple to use yet some 'Einstein' like ancestor must have had the patience and brains to set up such an accurate piece of apparatus, even if it was only used three times in every life time. Others believe that Parcymeirw field, next to the arrangement of stones, was the scene of a long forgotten battle, and the stones were raised to commemorate those who lost their lives. There is also a local legend that tells of 'Ladi Wen', a lady dressed in white who walks across the field on dark nights, and will kill anyone who ventures near the stones. The field is often covered with gossamer, except for the path which remains clear. Some locals will make a detour of a mile or more rather than cross the field at night.

Only one free standing, egg shaped ring, comprising of sixteen stones, exists in north Pembrokeshire today. This is on a level piece of moorland north of Mynachlog-ddu bridge and is called Gors Fawr Circle, and was still in use to work out the time of year in the 1950s. Shepherds would use the stars and the old 'circle' to time the gestation of their flocks.

CHAPTER TWO

The Shaping of Dyfed —
The Kingdom of Seven Cantref

Pembrokeshire was now home to a very mixed population, each with its own set of cultural traditions, but in 18,000 B.C., another tribe of people started to arrive in the county. These newcomers arrived from the east, from Holland and the Rhine, and differed in both appearance and customs to the Neolithic tomb-builders, who have now become known as the long-headed people who buried their dead in long barrows.

This race had rounded heads, was descended from the Northern warrior peoples who probably spoke a sort of Indo-European language. They were excellent archers, and came equipped with polished bronze battle axes and daggers.

These Bronze Age settlers, or Beaker Folk as they were called, buried their dead in round barrows, and placed stone decorated beakers in the graves with their dead — hence the name. These pottery beakers with delicately incised patterns, which had been made by using a wing bone of a blackbird as a chisel, contained a herb flavoured drink believed to sustain the deceased on the journey into the next world.

Sadly there are very few Beaker Folk settlements surviving today, suggesting that they were more nomadic than their predecessors. As little evidence remains, we can only surmise that the Beaker Folk lived mainly in skin tents or flimsy huts. We can assume too, that if they were nomadic, the women did not face the drudgery of the Neolithic woman, because they would collect few processions which needed cleaning. In fact, her lifestyle would have been better because preparing meat and milk foods was simpler than grinding corn and gathering fuel needed to sustain a diet based mainly on cereal.

Most characteristic of these people though is the fact that they buried their dead singly, and not in large communal long barrows as the Neolithic society had done. Beaker Chiefs, and their women, were buried individually, each body under its own mound, crouched on its side with the distinctive beaker and a few weapons and tools that would have represented their personal wealth at their side. At Corston Beacon a Beaker man was buried with a riveted bronze dagger at his side and at Kilpaison Burrows a barrow, exposed during a storm, revealed the body of a young woman who died around 1500 B.C.

There was obviously a gradual mix of Neolithic and Beaker Folk with intermarriage becoming more commonplace, and this could well account for the fact that round headed people have been found in long barrows and vice visa.

Under the influence of the Beaker Folk, the native settlers were beginning to learn new skills, the art of metal-working. The ore, which came mainly from the Wicklow Hills in Ireland, was worked into sheets by the Irish craftsman and imported to Britain and the continent. These invaders were quick to exploit the work of the Irish smiths, who were only too willing to supply them with daggers, axes and other small objects in bronze. Although these items were rare and costly, it helped to establish the use of bronze in Britain, and it appears that anyone who was anybody and wished to impress had an ornament made of Irish bronze or gold — similar to a status symbol today.

This was also a period when a new cultural society built religious temples, directed towards the sun and the heavens, for the first time throughout south-west Britain. The greatest remaining symbol of this era is at Stonehenge, which has dominated Salisbury Plain in Wiltshire for forty centuries. Pembrokeshire played a major role in the Stonehenge mystery when a Welsh geologist, H. H. Thomas, proved in 1923 that many of the bluestones (bluestone meaning holy stone — blue being a holy colour and a colour worn by Druids) that form the inner circle of Stonehenge came from the county. There have been many theories on this great pre-historic monument. Some say it was the work of giants, others

Reconstructed Round House Castell Henllys

Reconstructed animal shelter Castell Henllys

that it was the Temple of Druids. One historian even went as far as to say it was erected by Appalachian Indians, but whatever its purpose, how the stones reached Stonehenge remains one of the greatest mysteries of all times.

It all began when more than eighty stones were transported from the Preseli Hills to Salisbury Plain. A Professor R. J. C. Atkinson, who wrote the standard book 'Stonehenge', set out to prove the stones were hauled over land by sledge and rollers — probably as far as Canaston Bridge, and then taken by sea to Milford Haven. It has been suggested that at this point two pillars slipped from the rafts and local replacements hurriedly found, as it has been proven that the Alter Stone at Stonehenge, comes from the Llangwm area. The stones were then shipped along the Bristol Channel, up the River Avon and then by land to Warminster, down the River Wylye and on to their final resting place.

Mr Geoffrey Kellaway of the Institute of Geological Sciences has suggested that the bluestones were carried by glacier ice to within thirty miles of Stonehenge. This is based on the knowledge that the great Irish glacier flowed south-east up the Bristol Channel some 100,000 years ago carrying with it debris not only from Preseli, but from Ireland and Scotland too. Only recently was it discovered that this glacier overrode the Somerset coast and deposited part of its load in the Bristol-Bath region.

Stonehenge is supposed to be the work of many different people over a long period of time but the Preseli stones are thought to have been moved by the Beaker people between 1700 B.C. and 1650 B.C. It is possible that a temple had already been set up near Carn Menyn, where they originated, and that for some reason a Bronze Age tribe decided to move them to Wiltshire.

It has also been discovered that the circle of stones provide an accurate means of calculating the movements of the sun, moon, and major stars, during the year. In order to achieve this, the stones had to be set out to a high degree of accuracy, thus showing that primitive man had a good working knowledge of mathematics.

Whatever the theories and evidence concerning Stonehenge, I for one, would like to believe that our Beaker ancestors had more intelligence than we give them credit for, and were responsible for this tremendous feat.

The few cairns left by the Beaker folk in Pembrokeshire may seem pale in comparison to the splendour of Stonehenge but nevertheless they are still outstanding. These are usually situated on high ground, and often along the ancient trackway, the Flemings Way, used by the Bronze Age prospectors travelling between Wessex and Ireland. The three most interesting barrows, which come from the bluestone area, are a group of six barrows at Crugiau Cemais, and a group of three cairns that gives its name to Foel Drygarn.

There are many hut hollows in the county, which suggest that there were a number of large settlements. Recent excavations at Croes Mihangel have revealed a number of Bronze Age burial urns dating from 1500 B.C. Local legend states that criminals and lawbreakers were hanged here.

Crugiau Dwy has two cairns on its peak. Local legend tells the story that two women, some say goddesses, were in love with the same man, or god. They decided to go to the summit of Crugiau Dwy and fight a duel with stones, their lover acting as umpire. In the intense struggle to win their man both perished and the distraught lover gathered up the boulders they had fought with, and erected cairns on each grave.

Another fascinating site is on the St David's headland called Clawdd y Milwyr — The Warrior's Dyke. This is an enclosed settlement of about a dozen round huts and rock shelters which form a hillfort. The finds of spindle whorls and stone rubbers suggest that, although the area was barren and windswept, a community of farmers and stock breeders existed here.

Earlier hill-forts were protected only by a single curved bank, but by 100 B.C. double or even treble embankments were commonplace, suggesting that tribal battles and raiding were the main causes for concern. Examples of other headland forts can be seen at Bosherton Pools, Flimston Bay and Linney Head.

The Bronze Age was slowly being replaced by the Iron Age, when many groups of Celtic immigrants who had lived in what is now southern Germany and eastern France, began to settle. The oldest archaeological traces of the Celtic race can be found in the Austrian Alps at Halstatt, near Salzburg. They came to Britain via the sea-trading routes and spoke a language which is the forerunner of modern day Welsh. At Halstatt, we can see the first evidence of iron-working, the word 'iron' derives from the Celtic — isarnos. The Celts were constantly at war, being pressed from the north and east by the Germanic tribes, and the ever-expanding Roman Empire until they were forced to move to other lands, hence their arrival in Britain.

The Iron Age people were renowned for their great hill-fort building capabilities, the most spectacular to be found at Castell Henllys, situated to the west of Eglwyswrw. This fortified camp is in the process of being extensively excavated and restored, and will leave the visitor feeling as though he has entered a time-warp, giving an insight into the lives of these people.

Of all the invaders of Wales, it was the Celts who left the most permanent signs. Their settlements and hillforts are commonplace around the coast of Pembrokeshire, the largest Iron Age fort in West Wales is at Martin's Haven, and it is now assumed that the Haven provided a landing-place for the first Celtic settlers. The Celts were also believers in gods, and water — springs, rivers and lakes — were especially holy to them, hence the number of holy wells dotted around Wales.

Gradually, from about 500 B.C. onwards, these Celtic tribes grew in numbers, and extensive trading, together with people migration linked Wales and Ireland. Soon, because of its crucial position, Pembrokeshire became an important centre for the development of Celtic culture.

These early Celts brought with them a new proto-Celtic language which became divided into the Goedelic — the Irish, Gaelic and Manx languages, and the Brythonic — the Welsh, Cornish and Breton languages. It is from Brythonic that the modern Welsh of today is derived.

From this period too we inherit those wonderful stories that every Welsh child is spoon fed on — *Y Mabinogi* — a collection of stories that portray the mythological and colourful world of the old Celts. These stories are the oldest recorded Welsh tales, and were first written down in 1300 in *Llyfr Gwyn Rhydderch* ('The White Book of Rhydderch'), and again in the *Llyfr Coch Hergest* ('The Red Book of Hergest') between 1325 and 1425. The White Book is preserved in The National Museum of Wales, and The Red Book at Jesus College in Oxford.

These delightful stories are now considered masterpieces in medieval European literature. The Reverend John Jones, who took the Welsh bardic title Tegid, was born at Nevern. He transcribed The Red Book of Hergest so that Lady Charlotte Guest could translate the tales. An English

Model of Pwyll, Prince of Dyfed, Narberth

version, by Gwyn Jones and Thomas Jones, was published in Dent's Everyman's Library.

Arberth is the first place mentioned and tells the tale of Pwyll, Prince of Dyfed, and begins:

'Pwyll, Prince of Dyfed, was lord over the seven cantrefs of Dyfed, and once upon a time he was at Arberth, a chief court of his.'

In another section it mentions that he rose from a feast and 'made for the top of a mound which was above his court and called Gorsedd Arberth.'

According to one theory, Gorsedd Arberth was Sentence Castle at Templeton, where the Normans later built a castle ring.

Today the romantic stories of Pwyll are retold with colourful displays at the new Landsker Borderlands Visitor Centre situated in the historic Town Hall in the centre of Narberth, and are well worth a visit. The ruined Narberth Castle, which dates from 1246, the principal home of the local Welsh princes is also well worth a visit, and a walk along the Landsker borderlands trail will give you a feel for the enchanting life of Pwyll.

The next invaders of Wales were the Romans who had built a camp at Burrium, known as Usk today, to use as a base for their attacks upon the Silurian tribes of South Wales. They were present from 43 A.D. — 410 A.D. and it appears that, because the native inhabitants were content to live in their hill-forts and the Romans were more content to occupy the many valleys, Pembrokeshire seems not to have been troubled. Only one possible Roman camp site, used as a military post, has been discovered in Pembrokeshire. It was excavated by Sir Mortimer Wheeler, who found traces of a hypocaust — an Ancient Roman heating system, and fragments of Samian pottery, which suggests that the site was occupied during the second century A.D. Legend, however, prefers to tell us a different tale — that a table of gold lies buried there. In 1857, on land belonging to Baron de Rutzen, a hoard of Roman coins, weighing a hundredweight and wrapped in a skin, were found at Newton Farm. It is reported that the Baron gave the finder a cow in exchange for his treasure trove.

Although the Roman occupation was not strong in West Wales, it is believed they used slate ballast taken from the Preseli Hills to pave the wharves at Caerleon, their biggest settlement in Wales, and to repair the highways. It is also thought that the Roman ships patrolled the

Pembrokeshire coast against Irish sea-raiders, and may have set up a camp at Milford Haven. Interestingly though, in the autumn of 1859, a farmer digging a bog near Hanfeddau, in the parish of Clydau, came across a hoard of bronze swords and spearheads, most of which had been broken on purpose. Who knows, perhaps these were damaged intentionally to prevent approaching Romans from using them.

The Romans did however, know enough about the county to record its people as the Demetae, and Ptolemy referred to the land as Demetia, the Latin form of modern day Dyfed. They also left the Welsh one legacy, the leek, the national emblem of Wales. It is believed that it was they who introduced it into Wales, as leeks were commonly cultivated in Egypt in the time of the Pharaohs.

Harold Stone Bronze Age Fertility Stone

CHAPTER THREE

Christianity and Saintly Tales

Towards the end of the 4th, and the beginning of the 5th centuries, another group of invaders made their way to Pembrokeshire from a different direction. This time, it was the turn of an Irish tribe, the Deisi, who came from Deece in County Meath. Under the leadership of Eichaid Allmuir they settled in Pembrokeshire and ruled for several centuries.

They are best remembered in place-names and the Ogham writing on stones. These stones bear witness to the introduction of Christianity into Pembrokeshire long before it reached the rest of Britain. The Ogham alphabet was invented in Southern Ireland and consisted of up to five lines representing consonants, and dots representing the vowels. The characters were scratched on the corner of a pillar, the vowels being indented into the edge itself, and the lines etched either side or obliquely across. The inscription commonly runs from the bottom left-hand side and runs up the spine and down the other side of the stone. There are fifty-five known Ogham stones in Wales, and most can be found in the south-west. The Vitalianus stone outside the church at Nevern bears the Latin and Ogham inscription of Vitalianus Emeretus, who lived in the village during the 5th century. Another stone is inscribed *Maglocvni Fili Clvtori* in latin, and *Maglicunas Maqi Clutae* in Ogham, and is set into a windowsill inside the church. This is a monument to Maglocunus or Maelgwyn, the son of Clutorius or Clydor, who also lived in the 5th century. At St Dogmael's a stone which contains the dual inscription — *Sagrani Fili Cvnotami* in Latin, and *Sagrani Magi Cunatami* in Ogham, commemorates a local chieftain, Sagramus, the son of Cunolmus, who probably originated from Ireland. These stones are fine examples of memorials unique in Wales, but commonplace in Ireland. It was these stones that made it possible for the long forgotten script to be deciphered by a Victorian clergyman, Dr Graves, in 1848.

The early Christian community of South Wales was concerned with missionary work and these missionaries or 'saints' travelled between Ireland and the Continent to establish churches dedicated to them. This was also the age of Celtic crosses, and many of these are still to be found in Pembrokeshire. The most spectacular stands on the side of the road near the entrance to Carew Castle, and could have commemorated a gift of land to the church. It is decorated with plaits and knotwork, and the front contains a double panel. One side is inscribed — **Margiteut rex Etg Fili** — *Maredudd the king, son of Edwin.* Maredudd was a descendant of Hywel Dda, King of West Wales and the kingdom of Deheubarth. He and his brother, Hywel ab Edwin, obtained possession of Deheubarth in 1033, but two years later Maredudd was killed by the sons of Cynan. The other side of the panel is blank and it is believed that it was intended for commemorating his brother.

The high cross at Nevern is from the 11th century and is heavily decorated with panels and plaits, although the sculptor has made a mistake on one leg of the swastika on the front panel. Legend tells us that one day St David was carrying the thirteen foot stone cross on his shoulders and gave it to St Brynach in exchange for some bread. Although this is the land of enchantment there is little truth in this tale.

In another ancient legend we are told that a cuckoo would come on the 7th April each year, the feast day of St Brynach, and perch on the stone and sing. This was believed to be a religious duty among cuckoos, who selected one of their number to be God's messenger on that special day. For this reason it became a rule that the parish priest would not begin Mass on St Brynach's Day until the cuckoo-messenger appeared. One year the cuckoo was late and the priest and people waited patiently all day. Finally, they heard a feeble call among the yew trees, and then it arrived on the stone and uttered a faint note. The delighted congregation hurried inside to give thanks and celebrated Mass. When the villagers left the church they found the long journey had been too much for the cuckoo, and it lay dead at the foot of the cross.

Yew trees were planted inside the churchyard for safety, because they were considered to make the best longbows, which were used to such a great effect at Crecy and Agincourt.

Another interesting legend concerns the second yew tree on the right as one enters the churchyard. Seven feet from the ground there is a deep gash, from which a tacky substance strongly resembling blood weeps out. Tradition states that a monk was charged with a terrible crime, although the nature of the crime has been long forgotten. He protested his innocence, but he was nevertheless condemned to death and hung from the tree. In desperation the monk claimed that 'If you hang me, guiltless as I am, this tree will bleed for me.'

The most famous of all Pembrokeshire's saintly figures is Dewi Sant, St David, patron saint of Wales. But the first legend concerning St David began some thirty years before his birth. Tradition states that St Patrick, patron saint of Ireland, who was possibly a Pembrokeshire man himself, came to St David's and stood on the place where the Cathedral now stands. He thought this to be an ideal place and vowed that he would serve God there. However, a heavenly vision told him that the place had been reserved for another person to be born in thirty years time. Deeply disappointed St Patrick went down to Whitesands Bay and looking towards Ireland decided to serve God there. It is said that before St Patrick sailed for Ireland he raised from the dead a man called Criumther, who had been dead for forty years. Criumther went with St Patrick to Ireland where he later became a bishop.

Before we learn a little about Saint David, perhaps we should mention his mother, Nonita or St Non. There are many legends surrounding St David's birth, but they all basically tell the same tale. A divine power sent Sanctus, the king of Ceredigion, to Dyfed, and there he saw a beautiful young nun called Nonita. He was immediately attracted to her and took her by force, conceiving a child, which was later to become St David. Nonita, who was a virgin before this encounter, continued to live a life of chastity, existing on bread and water. When the child was due to be born, she returned to the field where she had conceived. Although a violent storm was raging, when she arrived at the place of conception, it was a summer's day with sunshine and blue skies. In the throes of childbirth pain Nonita supported herself on a stone and it is said that the stone bears the mark of her hand. The stone then broke in two in sympathy with the

St Govan's Chapel

agony of the young mother-to-be. Legend also tells us that at the moment of St David's birth, a spring of the purest water burst from the earth to salute the birth of the holy child. Today the well, which is about a kilometre from Britain's smallest city, St Davids, is well cared for with a statuette of Our Lady in a niche opposite. Later, in 520, a chapel was built on the site, with the pieces of cracked stone embedded in its foundations. The stone beneath the altar bears some marks which some say are the marks of St Non's fingers in her hour of labour, but it is more likely that these are traces of an Ogham inscription.

David's paternal grandmother was Meleri, daughter of the Irish Lord Brychan Brycheiniog of Brecknock, and his mother Non could trace her ancestry to the Irish aristocracy. He was baptised by a blind monk named Movi at Porth Clais, and legend states that a spring appeared and Movi was cured of his blindness. David was taught by Paulinus, who was blinded apparently through 'much weeping', and he is credited with restoring his sight too.

David established his home at Tŷ Gwyn, the white house or holy house, and it is said that his followers were attracted by his strict austere life. He was known as Dewi Ddyfrwr, *David the Waterdrinker*, the first teetotaller in Welsh history. An early Breton chronicle refers to him as *'aquaticus'* which suggests that he was a member of a monastic set that rejoiced in a rigorous life and were known as the watermen. He was also a strict vegetarian and leeks, the emblem of Wales, were a staple ingredient of his diet.

In 519 the so-called Victory Synod was held at Llanddewi Brefi, in Cardigan. Pelagius was attempting to deny the doctrine of original sin and David was called to the meeting because the leaders were failing to crush the Celtic preacher's heresy. It is said that he went reluctantly to the meeting which, in fact, was a preaching contest for the title of archbishop. Nobody could make his voice heard until a white dove flew down and rested on St David's shoulder. As he began to speak, the ground rose into a hillock and, 'his voice rang out like a trumpet, so that all could hear clearly.' His speech was so well-delivered that the bishops and abbots were spell-bound. They immediately stepped forward and asked him to become their primate. He agreed on condition that the see was moved from Caerleon to his own district.

St David was at his most awesome when he encountered the Irish chieftain Boia. Boia was annoyed at the smoke rising from St David's settlement and, encouraged by his wife, set out with his men to kill the monks. On their way they were stricken with a mysterious fever and were unable to carry out their evil deeds, even the cattle were struck down. Finally Boia said to David. 'The land shall be yours for ever.' St David took compassion on the man and brought his cattle to life, but Boia's wife was 'afire with jealous spite'. She instructed her maids to lead the monks into a life of sin by stripping naked, 'playing games and using lewd language' in front of them. The maids did as they were told imitating sexual intercourse and sexual embraces, but St David and his monks remained strong. It is said that on this site the monastery was built and that St David made the monks toil at daily labour with their hands, heads bent to prevent temptation.

David lived to be a very old man and died on the 1st March, 589. He was canonized, at the request of Henry I, by Pope Calixtus II in 1120. The present cathedral, the largest in Wales, was begun in 1180 and a new

Carew Cross

shrine, where St David's relics are kept in a portable casket, was built in 1275.

St Govan's chapel wedged between the rocks below St Govan's Head is surrounded by legends. It is constructed of local stone and topped with a slate roof. Fifty-two limestone steps lead down to the chapel, but never the same number to ascend. It is a single chamber with an earthen floor, and an altar with a cleft in the rock behind it. It is said that St Govan hid there when pirates from Lundy Island came to ransack his church. Local tradition relates that the recess closed around him, hiding him from the pillagers. The empty bellcote once housed a silver bell, which legend tells us was stolen by pirates, but no sooner had the thieves set sail, than the

The Bleeding Yew Tree at Nevern

boat was wrecked and all hands were lost. Sea-nymphs returned the bell and placed it in a bell rock outside the chapel, where it now lies encased in rock. It is reputed that when St Govan tapped the rock the bell would ring a thousand times stronger than the original bell.

A traditional verse tells of the bell;

There is nothing to hope and nothing to fear
When the wind sounds low on Bosherston Mere
There is much to fear and little to hope
When unseen hands pull St Govan's rope
And the magic stones, as the wise know well
Promise sorrow and death, like St Govan's bell.

The Vitalianus Stone

Who St Govan was remains a puzzle. Some believe that he was Gobham, a contemporary of St David, who founded the abbey of Dairnis, near Wexford, who died in 586 A.D. and is believed to be buried beneath the altar. Others say it is the cell of the Arthurian knight Gawaine of the Round Table, who became a hermit after the death of King Arthur. Others believe that it is the cell of St Gofen, wife of a Celtic chief.

The age of the cell is unknown, but historians believe that it wasn't built until the 13th century. Interestingly, Gerald of Wales does not mention it in his *Description of Wales*, written in 1188, which if it had existed, he would have certainly mentioned it. Another contemporary of St David was St Justinian, one of the first Christians to preach in Wales, who built

Statuette of Our Lady St Non's

himself a cell on Ynys Dyfanog, *Ramsey Island* to escape the negligent ways of the mainland monks. St Justinian was murdered on the island and it is said that he walked across the 'sound' carrying his severed head under his arm. He placed it on the opposite shore, and his chapel was built on the spot.

Another interesting tale regarding a head, is the story of St Teilo's Skull. When St Teilo was on his death-bed he told his maidservant that one year after his burial she was to take his skull to Llandeilo Llwydarth and place it beside a spring of clear water so that sick people could drink the waters from his skull, and be cured of their ailments.

Even as late as 1850, sick people were flocking to the well to be cured, but in order for the cure to work, the skull had to be filled with water by a member of the Melchior family — descendants of the maidservant. At the turn of this century, Miss Melchior, the last of the family sold the skull for £50 to a person who claimed to be acting on behalf of Llandaf Cathedral, and it has never been seen or heard of since.

It is claimed that St Teilo is buried in three places, Llandaf, Llandeilo Fawr in Carmarthen and Llandeilo Llwydarth, near Maenclochog in north Pembrokeshire. Legend recalls that when St Teilo died all three churches requested his body for burial. After much discussion it was agreed to spend a day and a night in prayer. When morning arrived, instead of one body, there were three, so everyone was happy.

Another interesting story concerns St Teilo and the ancient village of Mathri and is told in *The Book of Llandaf*. It is said that the wife of Cynwayw, a man of Daugleddau, had septuplet sons and the distraught father, who could not afford to provide for his instant family, decided to drown them in the river like unwanted kittens. As he was about to perform this act St Teilo passed and saved the children and promised to bring them up in the church. For their daily food, 7 large fishes appeared at the water's edge — hence the name Ddyfrwr, *the Watermen*, by which the septuplets became known. They settled in Mathri and became known as the 'Seven Saints of Mathri'. When they died they were interred in stone coffins which were visible in the churchyard until 1720. *The Book of Llandaf* explains that the name of the village comes from the Latin word *martyrium*, meaning martyrs. Others say its origins derive from the Welsh words Ma-thri — meaning the field of woe.

Another ancient holy well with an interesting legend was once situated in the churchyard at St Edren's, between Haverfordwest and Croesgoch. It was said that the waters could cure madness but, according to the legend, the well dried up because a woman washed clothes in it on a Sunday. Anyway the magic of the water was supposed to have been transferred to grass growing around the church. If it was made into a sandwich with bread, and money placed in a stone in the church wall, the grass was reputed to cure hydrophobia.

The mid to late 17th century was notable for its rise in religious dissenters, those who refused to confirm to the established church.

When William Laud, a former Bishop of St David's, became Archbishop of Canterbury in 1633, non-conformist clergy began to hold meetings in private houses to avoid persecution. One such house on St Thomas' Green was known as the 'Green Meeting House'. In 1651 a small chapel was built on an adjoining site and became the mother church of nonconformity in Pembrokeshire. It was restored in 1841 and renamed Albany Independent Chapel.

The Quakers established themselves at Haverfordwest around 1630 and a number of dissenters were persecuted for holding unlawful meetings. Some emigrated to Pennsylvania. This came about when Lewis David, one of the trustees of the Company of Adventurers purchased land for £60 from William Penn in 1681, feeling that the Pembrokeshire Quakers would be able to settle and keep their customs and language. The land was then re-sold in smaller lots to individuals with Pembrokeshire connections and established towns such as Haverford and Narbeth in North America.

The Baptist church was established in 1668 at Rhydwilym by a faithful few under Reverend William Jones, a dissenting vicar of Cilymaenllwyd. The early Baptists were mainly wealthy well-educated pillars of society, but Reverend Jones recruited his followers from the peasants who were poorly educated. By 1689 he had 113 followers. In 1701, at his own expense, John Evans built the first chapel on its present site in Rhydwilym and, as now, its members were baptised in the river that flows besides the chapel. It was from this chapel that the first persecuted Baptists travelled to America and established the First Baptist Church of America.

A Welsh custom, invented in the days before people could read, was the *Pwnc* Festival, which was held on Whit Monday in chapels throughout Pembrokeshire. Today it is still sung in Rhydwilym Chapel at Whitsuntide. A *pwnc*, which means 'subject', is a selected chapter of the Old Testament translated into Welsh, learnt by heart, and rehearsed for the festival. Those gathered would chant the opening verse together, followed first by the young girls then the boys. Then in turn by the male and female adult members, followed by the elderly ladies and men. All the neighbouring chapels would attend the festival, vying with each other for perfection. Authorities now believe that the chant which has an ancient 13/8 signature with quarter tones is remnants of Iron Age music, which could mean that this is an ancient custom handed down from that period.

Albany Chapel, Haverfordwest

Rhydwilym Baptist Church

CHAPTER FOUR

The Vikings, The Normans, and Little England Beyond Wales

The later part of the Christian Era was disrupted by the Vikings who had little respect for Christianity, St David, or the people of Pembrokeshire. The Vikings raided the coast on many occasions between 844 and 1091 A.D. using Milford Haven as a temporary base and burning St David's on eight separate occasions. In the year 877, a chieftain called Hubba, after whom Hubberston was named, is said to have been forced to 'winter' in the haven with a fleet of 23 ships and 2,000 warriors. We can assume that this had quite an effect on the local community life, and the birth-rate too! It is interesting to note that, according to a survey carried out by the Blood Transfusion Service 33% of south Pembrokeshire people have the A gene blood group — the same as many southern Scandinavian races today — the home of yesterday's early Vikings.

The Vikings are credited with giving Pembrokeshire another legacy too — the Pembrokeshire Corgi, reputed to have descended from the Swedish Vallund, which was introduced into Wales by the Viking raiders who settled here. The animal was certainly mentioned in the Welsh Laws of Hywel Dda.

The great Olaf Haroldston also invaded the shire in 1091. Some historians believe that there were a considerable number of Viking settlements in the area around 1100 A.D. Although there are at least 21 place names of Norse derivation — Skokholm, Skomer, and Goodwick to name but a few, there is no reliable archaeological evidence to prove this. Caldy, the cold island, is another. However, for centuries before they

Roch Castle

arrived Caldy was known as Ynys Bŷr, the *island of Pŷr*, who is said to have established a monastery there. Legend tells us that Pŷr died after falling into a pond in a drunken stupor and was succeeded as abbot by Samson, who was sanctified as bishop in 521 and later travelled in Cornwall and Ireland before settling in Dol in Brittany.

The death of Rhys ap Tewdwr, in 1092, the last prince of South Wales, triggered the most important event in the history of Pembrokeshire. The Welsh tribes of Deheubarth, already weakened by their own conflicts, became easy prey to the advancing Norman armies. By the end of the year, Roger of Montgomery and his son Arnulph had overrun south Pembrokeshire and chose the rocky peninsula where Pembroke castle now stands as their base. The Welsh chieftains now had a common enemy, and attempts were made to keep the intruders out. Earthworks were constructed over the southern part of the county, but gradually the land came under the rule of the invaders. By the first half of the twelfth century over 50 castles, most no more than earthworks, were built. These developed into more substantial motte and bailey forts, which in turn evolved into stone castles, and can be seen dotted around the county. They were usually built near the water to maintain supplies and reinforcements. Among these was Pembroke Castle, which at the time was one of the largest and strongest fortresses in the Kingdom. The castle was built on a site that may well have been used by the Romans, as Roman coins have been found, although few other relics.

When Arnulph returned to England, he left the fortress in the charge of Gerald of Windsor, but as soon as the Norman left, the Welsh leaders gathered their men to storm the castle. The initial attack was beaten back, so the Welsh planned a seige hoping to starve the garrison into surrender. Both sat patiently waiting for the other to give up until eventually it was a clever move on the part of the Normans that ended the seige. When they were down to their last four flitches of bacon, Gerald decided to take a gamble in an attempt to conclude matters. He ordered his men to throw the bacon to the Welsh besiegers and shouted that, as the garrison had plenty to sustain them for a long period, they would have more need for them. In case the French Normans were misunderstood, Gerald wrote a note to Arnulph saying that his men were in excellent spirits and had enough food to sustain them for as long as it was necessary to hold out. A messenger was then instructed to 'accidentally' lose the note where the Welsh would find it. As expected it was picked up and taken to the Bishop of St David's who translated it from French to Welsh. The Welsh, now convinced they were fighting a lost cause, returned home. It can be said that the division of Pembrokeshire, 'Little England Beyond Wales' — The Landsker — was born on that day.

During the next two centuries the Normans erected a chain of castles marking the boundary between hill and bog, behind which, the Welsh retreated and made a living from the rugged land. The Landsker, or frontier, can today be traced through a line of strongholds, castles and churches straddling south Pembrokeshire and Cardiganshire.

The Welsh never forgot how they were deceived by Gerald of Windsor and vowed to get their revenge. Meanwhile Henry I had commandeered the lands of the Montgomery family who had rebelled against the King, but Gerald retained his position as custodian of the castle and, on the orders of the King married Nest, Helen of Wales, the Welsh Helen of Troy. One day Owain ap Cadwgan, the son of Cadwgan, saw Nest at an Eisteddfod in Cardigan and decided that her Welsh beauty should not be wasted on a foreigner, and was determined to claim Nest for himself. He gathered a small band of men together and, at Christmas 1105, stormed the castle of Earwere (now Amroth), burnt it down and kidnapped Nest and her children. When the King heard of this he was furious because Nest had once been a mistress of the King and had a child by him. Owain fled to Ireland but, because he was a skilful soldier, was eventually allowed to return to fight against Gruffudd, son of Rhys ap Tewdwr, as the Welsh leader against the Normans.

By 1096 the native people made an attempt to reclaim south Pembrokeshire but failed. Pembroke then became the principality of Gilbert de Clare who, in 1138, became Earl of Pembroke, when the town became a county palatine. This means that the Earl had certain privileges and authority to act like a king, so the county had no representative in Parliament.

The unique division between the 'Englishry' of the south of the country, and the 'Welshry' of the north was now well underway. The Normans, who originally descended from the Northmen and not the French, mingled with the Norse colonists, helped by the close kinship with each other in their opposition to the Welsh.

Meanwhile, in 1108 part of the low-lying land of Flanders had been drowned by the sea and many people made homeless. On hearing this, Henry I encouraged a group of Flemish refugees to settle in south Pembrokeshire as a defence against 'the unquiet Welshmen'. The first party of Flemings to arrive landed at Mun's Mouth, in Milford Haven, and included Alexander de Rudepac, who was nicknamed 'Wizo'. Henry I granted him the lordship of Daugleddau, the area between the Western and Eastern Cleddau rivers. It is said that Wizo gave advowson of the church at Rudbaxton, to the Knights Hospitallers of St John of Jerusalem at Selbach in the early part of the 12th century. The Knights came about after the first crusade and recapture of Jerusalem in 1099. They cared for the wounded and when the crusade was over some settled in Pembrokeshire to carry on their good work. Wizo the Fleming gave money to support the churches and founded a strong army in south Pembrokeshire who were often called upon by the King to fight against the Welsh Princes, so learning to both fear and hate the Welsh. These immigrants from Flanders were a hardy race who were experts in commerce and the manufacture of woollen goods, the remnants of this thriving trade can be seen today in a few surviving mills.

When Wizo died, it is said that there were many claimants to his estate at Castell Gwys, *Wiston* near Haverfordwest and an interesting legend has grown around it. A basilisk, or monster, lived near Wiston Bank. Although quite small, about a foot in length, it was a reptile with a black and yellow skin, with eyes in the back of its head as well as the front. It was feared by everyone because it was reputed to be able to kill anyone with its threatening gaze. However, if a human being saw the monster without being seen, it would die, and so it was decided that anyone who could look at the basilisk without being seen should inherit the estate. Of course there were many claimants, but none lived long enough to collect their inheritance, until one day an enterprising young man had an idea. He took a barrel to the top of the hill, got inside and rolled down the hill past the spot where the monster lived. As he passed by he looked through the bung and called 'I can see you, but you can't see me', and, it is said, from that day he became the proud owner of the Wiston estate.

More Flemings settled in the area in 1111, and again in 1156 at Rhos and Daugleddau where they worked as farmers within a feudal system.

Roch Castle occupies a solitary position on the summit of a rocky outcrops and was built during the 12th century by the feudal lord, Adam de la Roche. According to legend a witch told him that his death would be caused by a *gwiber*, viper, but if he lived a full year he would be safe and need never worry again. Immediately he ordered a stronghold to be built on its present site, well out of the reach of the snake. Lord Roche moved to the top floor and remained there, in constant fear, until the last day of the year. Because it was bitterly cold, he sent one of his servants to collect a basket full of firewood so that he could at least enjoy the comforts of a blazing fire on his last evening in captivity. As he was putting the logs onto

11th Century Keep Wiston

Pembroke Castle

the fire an adder crawled out of the basket and bit him. The following morning he was found dead in front of the hearth.

Roch castle was later occupied by Lucy Walters, mistress of Charles II, and she spent most of her childhood here. The castle is now used as self catering accommodation for tourists, and many claim to have seen the ghost of a slim built Lucy, clad in a white dress, appearing at windows and floating through locked doors.

CHAPTER FIVE

The Tudors in Pembroke

The Tudor period began when Henry Tudor, Earl of Richmond, returned to his native country. As he set foot on Welsh soil at Mill Bay, near Dale, at sunset on Sunday 7th August 1485 he unfurled his banner bearing the Red Dragon of the ancient hero Cadwaladr. The motto on the present day Welsh flag, **y ddraig goch ddyry gychwyn** — *the red dragon made the start* — derives from a poem that was presented to Henry by Deio ap Ieuan Ddu, and dates from this period.

The precise landing spot is unknown, but local tradition claims that Harry's Carthouse is the exact spot, and maintains that Henry complained that the cliff path was 'brunt', meaning steep, giving the name to the farm above the bay.

Early the following morning Henry and his uncle set off crossing Mullock Bridge where, according to legend, Sir Rhys ap Thomas, the valiant Welshman, was hiding under an arch to release him from an oath that he had sworn to King Richard III. When Richard become aware of the Henry Tudor's intention to dispute his right to the throne, he sent his commissioners to the neighbouring town of Carmarthen to administer the oath of allegiance. Sir Rhys had promised to be faithful to the King 'whoever ill-affected to the State shall dare to land in those parts of Wales where I have employment under your Majesty must resolve with himself to make his entrance and irruption over by body.' Sir Rhys was troubled by the promise and so he consulted the Bishop of St David's who advised that Henry Tudor could not be looked upon as 'ill-affected to the State' because he came to relieve the country of an unrighteous ruler. The oath was, therefore, void.

Sir Rhys took 8,000 soldiers to march with Henry to Bosworth Field and, after welcoming him, Sir Rhys, who was still not happy with the Bishop's advice, took the additional precaution of lying beneath the bridge so that the future king could walk over his body.

Henry marched through Haverfordwest, across the Preseli mountains, where it is said he stayed the night at Fegwyr Lwyd, near Cilgwyn then on to Cardigan, Machynlleth, Shrewsbury, Lichfield and finally on to Bosworth Field in Leicestershire.

It is said that it was from Sir Rhys that Richard III received his fatal wounds, and it was he who placed the muddy crown of England, which had rolled into a thorn bush, on the head of the new King. This could be true, because it is said that the King Henry knighted him on the battlefield with the sword that still bore the blood of the late King Richard. From that day onwards the King always called him 'Father Rhys'.

Henry Tudor was born on 28th January, 1457, at Pembroke Castle, just three months after the death of his father. His mother, Margaret Beaufort, the fourteen year old daughter of the Earl of Somerset, was taken for protection to Pembroke Castle by Saipar Tudur, Jasper Tudor, Earl of Pembroke, whilst Edmund, her husband, was fighting in the Wars of the Roses. In 1456, Edmund was imprisoned at Carmarthen, and although released within a couple of days, he died a few weeks later of T.B. probably picked up whilst in custody. He was buried at Grey Friars at Carmarthen but when his grandson, Henry VIII, dissolved the monasteries, his body was moved to St David's Cathedral, where his tomb stands before the high altar.

When his mother remarried Henry was left in the care of his uncle Jasper but, in 1471, after the Lancastrian failure at Tewkesbury, Jasper and his nephew, set sail from Tenby and escaped to Brittany. It was there, fourteen years later, that they planned the landing that would eventually lead him to Westminster to be crowned King and thus begin the Tudor Dynasty.

By now Margaret Beaufort had married her third husband Thomas, Lord Stanley, who, as one of the greatest men at the Yorkist court, become the guardian of Princess Elizabeth when Edward IV died. Although Britain came under the rule of the Yorkists, there was much unrest and attempts had been made to over throw Richard III. Under the

Mill Bay, St Anne's Head

Brunt Farm

influence of Margaret and John Mostin, Bishop of Ely, it was decided to support Henry in a bid for the throne for the House of Lancaster. After much discussion, a Welsh doctor slipped unnoticed passed Elizabeth's guards, and persuaded her to marry Henry Tudor if he defeated Richard III.

On Christmas Day 1483, in Rennes Cathedral, Henry Tudor stood before his court and proclaimed himself King Henry VII, and promised to marry Princess Elizabeth as soon as he had secured the throne, a promise fulfilled on 18th January 1486.

Henry VII had a strong affection for Wales, and anything Welsh, hardly surprising when you consider that he was nursed by a Welsh foster-mother, and spoke the native language. He had a passion for Welsh history and genealogy, and employed the best genealogist in the country to establish the ancestry of his grandfather Owain Tudor. He even named his eldest child Arthur, after the legendary figure whom every Welshman in the land was looking forward to the day when 'Arthur the once and future King' would return. It was from this old Welsh prophecy that Henry hoped to gain the love and respect of his fellow countrymen, but it was not to be the case. Catherine of Spain married Arthur, but Arthur was not strong and within a year he died. Henry was broken hearted but determined to keep the Tudor dynasty going. After a special edict from the Pope, the newly widowed Catherine of Aragon was married to Arthur's younger brother Henry and became the first of the six wives of the future Henry VIII.

The king wore fabulous clothes and jewels, and for the first time the word majesty entered the English language to describe him. He also started the Yeoman of the Guard, the first standing army in England, although at the time there were only 150 of them.

There were many Welshmen in his court and he always observed St David's Day. Records show that he gave the Welshmen in his court £2.00 to celebrate their national day in 1492. The day ended with a traditional Noson Lawen — an evening's entertainment of poetry, song and dance. Henry's grand-daughter, Queen Elizabeth I, the last of the Tudors, had a special affinity with Wales too. She authorised the use of the Welsh Prayer Book and a Welsh Bible, at a time when she was trying to impose a single religious standard throughout the land.

Tudor Merchant's House Tenby

One hundred years after Henry VII died at Richmond, the Welsh writer, George Owen, recorded in his *Description of Pembrokeshire*, that the dying King commanded of his son, who was to become Henry VIII, 'that he should have a special care for his own nation and countrymen, the Welshmen.' But Henry VIII soon forgot his promises to his father because in 1536 he abolished the privilege of County Palatine to Haverfordwest and Pembroke to unite them with other lordships, forming the old thirteen counties of Wales.

Although Pembrokeshire has been a sea-trading county from the earliest days, it wasn't until the 15th and 16th centuries that the shire became alive with activity as fleets of ketches, sailing ships and barges, manouvered in and out of the various ports and harbours.

The Tudor period was probably the time of Tenby's greatest importance and in 1457, the year of Henry VII's birth, the Earl of Pembrokeshire helped the inhabitants to rebuild and strengthen the walls of the town against the coming of the Spanish Armada. However, by 1588, the walls were once again in need of repair. There are two most interesting houses dating from this period in Tenby today. One, the Tudor Merchant's House on Quay Hill, has a fine example of a gabled front and a corbelled chimney-breast. The ground floor is now open as a museum. The other, next door, is Plantagenet House.

One of the greatest men of the Tudor period, Robert Recorde was born in Tenby in about 1510. He was the pioneer of mathematical writers in the country and was first to introduce the knowledge of algebra into Britain, the first writer of geometry and astronomy, the inventor of the present method of finding the square root, and the inventor of the equal (=) sign, which is now used throughout the world. In 1525 he went to All Souls, Oxford where he studied and later lectured in mathematics, music and anatomy at the college. His first book, entitled *The Grounde of Arts — a popular arithmetic*, was published in 1543. At Cambridge University he took a medical degree in 1545, and it is thought that in 1547 he became physician to the young King Edward VI and Queen Mary.

In 1548, he was asked by the Privy Council, either because he was a distinguished doctor or because he was a good judge of character, to interview a prisoner, named Allen, who was confined in the Tower of London. Allen persistently claimed that he was a prophet and the authorities believed he was feigning insanity. Sadly the outcome was not recorded, but the following year we find Recorde as Comptroller of the Mint in Bristol, and within a few years surveyor of the mines in England and Ireland, so perhaps the authorities received the answer they were looking for.

His book, *The Castle of Knowledge*, which concerns astronomy and was written in the form of a dialogue between master and pupil, contains the following quatrains in the preface:

54

Five Arches Tenby

If reasons reache transcende the Skye
Why should it then to earth be bounde?
The witte is wronged and leadde awyre,
If mynde be married to the grounde.

The book contains 182 pages, and the title page shows a castle in the centre with people looking towards the heights of the stars. Obviously one of Pembrokeshire's castles influenced the design of his woodcut, but alas no records exists to inform us of which one. Interestingly a copy of this book, together with another on mathematics fetched the sum of 3s 6d (17½p) at a London auction sale in 1664. In 1960 a copy of Castle of Knowledge alone was sold by Sotheby's of London for £1,100.

Recorde was later summoned before the Court of the King's Bench on a charge of 'defamation of magnates' and ordered to pay £1,000 with costs — a vast sum in those days. Unable to pay the fine, he was placed in Southwark prison, where it is believed he died.

The last days of Robert Recorde's life are shrouded in as much mystery as the sculptured head on a pillar in Tenby parish church. The plaque was modelled in 1909 by Owen Thomas from a dilapidated early 17th century oil painting discovered over 100 years ago in Middlesex and reputed to be that of the Tenby genius. The person is shown bareheaded, bald, and wearing a black dress. The painting has been badly damaged by over-cleaning, and the inscription 'Robt Record M.D. 1556' is thought to have been added much later, possibly in the 19th century.

CHAPTER SIX

The Civil War and Beyond

Just as the Landsker had divided the county of Pembrokeshire, so did the Civil War. In the north, Welsh Pembrokeshire was staunchly Royalist, whilst the anglicized south favoured the views of the Parliamentarians, although there were many changes of loyalty on, both sides, before the Restoration of Charles II.

In 1644 the Royalist Earl Carbery, who lived at Golden Grove in Carmarthenshire, attempted to break Pembroke but he was driven back by Colonel Rowland Laugharne, at that time Parliamentary leader. He claimed Tenby, Haverfordwest and Carmarthen from the Royalists forcing them to replace their leader in West Wales. After a determined assault on the area the Royalists recaptured Haverfordwest and Carmarthen. It has been recorded that Laugharne was 'one of the ablest tacticians thrown up during the unhappy conflict'.

The most famous local battle of the first Civil War occurred on 1st August 1645 at Colby Moor, a rough patch of moorland between Wiston and Llawhaden. Three days earlier Major General Rowland Laugharne assembled his army at Canaston Woods and marched to the moor where they met the Royalist Army from Haverfordwest. Although there was total confusion, it was to be the major's greatest hour, and signalled the beginning of the end for the Royalist cause in Wales. 150 Royalists were killed and a total of 700 men taken prisoner. To this day, Pembrokeshire folk refer to a state of confusion as a 'Colby Moor Rout'.

Interestingly, when the parish church of Wiston was being restored in 1864, three cartloads of human bones were discovered buried beneath the pews. It is assumed that these were the remains of the unfortunate victims slain at that disastrous battle.

In the same year Laugharne seized for the Cromwellians, Roch Castle, home of William Walter. However, four months later it was retaken by the King's men. William Walter claimed his property, sheep and cattle had suffered greatly during these exchanges and so he went to London to submit a claim for £3,000 compensation. On this occasion his seventeen year old daughter, Lucy, accompanied him and, it is said, met the Prince of Wales, later Charles II, for the first time.

The following year Lucy was taken to Holland by her aunt, Mary Gosfright, who was married to a Dutchman. At The Hague, it is claimed, Lucy became the mistress of Charles and their affair is well documented. On 9th April 1649, at Rotterdam, she gave birth to James, later Duke of Monmouth. In July and August of that year Charles and Lucy stayed in Paris and St Germain. However, in 1650, whilst Charles was in Scotland, she had an affair with the future Earl of Arlington, by whom she had a daughter Mary.

In 1656 Lucy returned to England where she was arrested and charged with being a spy. She was imprisoned in the Tower of London but a month later discharged when Parliament decided to exile 'Charles Stuart's lady of pleasure and the young heir'. She returned to Holland, and then made her way back to Paris where in 1658 she died of typhoid. Charles recognised Lucy's son as the eldest of his illegitimate children and it would appear he was the favourite. Even the diarist Samuel Pepys observed that the king 'did doat upon his son,' bestowing many honours, including the Order of the Garter.

A rumour spread throughout the land that Charles and Lucy had been legally married, but the king strenuously denied this on three separate occasions. An intriguing mystery that occurred in Pembrokeshire during the middle of the following century may be related to the royal affair.

The Home Office issued a warrant demanding the marriage register for the district of St Thomas, Haverfordwest, to be sent to London. No reason was given, but more significantly, the records were never returned. This could have been a genuine oversight on the part of the Home Office, or perhaps there was a more sinister reason. If the register

Colby Moor scene of the Civil War Battle of Colby

had contained the solemnised marriage of Lucy Walter to Charles Stuart it would have affected the right of the House of Hanover to lay claim to the throne because Charles died without an heir. Sadly we shall never know the truth.

Oliver Cromwell came to Pembrokeshire in 1648 with the main aim of destroying Pembroke castle. He left London on 3rd May, and arrived in Carmarthen, in the neighbouring county, on 22nd May. His course took him passed Killanow Toll gate, through Merrixton Lane, and down the Old Welsh Road, passing Camomile Bank Inn, so named because of the camomile that grows in profusion around it, and is reputed to be over 400 years old. He continued over Stepaside Brook before making his way to Tenby. Legend tells us that it was at Camomile Bank Inn that Cromwell give the order for his men to 'step aside' — meaning to step out of the line of march and take some rest and refreshment. Since that day, estimated to be 23rd May 1648, the little hamlet has been known as Stepaside. Just eight days later Tenby surrendered.

At Pembroke Colonel John Poyer, Colonel Rice Powell and Major-General Rowland Laugharne, gathered forces to march eastward where they fought the Roundheads, under Horton, and were defeated. Poyer, Powell and Laugharne were condemned to death for treason, but Cromwell declared that only one sentence should be carried out. To decide the issue three pieces of paper were placed in a hat, two inscribed 'Life Given of God', and the third blank. A child was ordered to draw the lot, Poyer drew the blank and was shot at Covent Garden on 25 April 1649. When Charles II was restored to the throne he granted Poyer's widow a good pension.

The town of Haverfordwest was left 'destitute and depleted' as a result of military occupation during the Civil war, and it came to grief again in 1652 when the inhabitants suffered an outbreak of plague. Over three hundred of its residents died, and prayers were even said in some London churches for 'the stricken folk of Haverfordwest'.

After the Civil War there were no more major battles until Wales became the scene of the last invasion of Britain, an incident which is often referred to as a battle — The Battle of Fishguard. As the result of this event the Pembroke Yeomanry were allowed to wear the Fishguard Battle honours.

On 16 February 1797 an army, under the command of Colonel William Tate, sailed from Brest under the Russian flag, with orders to burn and destroy Bristol, then England's second largest city. The army consisted of six hundred regulars, and eight hundred convicts released from the French jails, along with one hundred emigres who were captured at Quiberon and three Irish Officers. They were armed with muskets and cutlasses and, because their uniforms were dyed black, they were known as *La Legion Noire* — the Black Legion.

Because of storms they were unable to land and made their way around the coast intending to land the troops at Cardigan Bay and march to Chester and Liverpool. By mid-day four ships, the *Resistance*, the *Constance*, the *Vengeance* and the *Vautour*, now flying the British colours, were sighted off Bishop Rock by Thomas Williams of Treleddyn, who being a master mariner suspected that they were French. The squadron anchored at Carreg Wastad and the troops and supplies were discharged. Meanwhile, the *Vautour*, sailed on but, after being fired at, returned with the news that Fishguard was heavily guarded.

The sloop, *Britannia*, under the command of John Owen was in the area

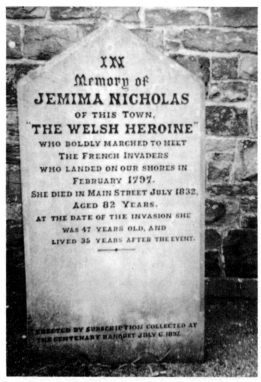

Gravestone of Jemima Nicholas — The Welsh Heroine

carrying a cargo of culm from Hook. It was stopped by the *Vengeance*, and Owen was taken on board and, during interrogation, gave an exaggerated account of the port's heavy defence. Whilst on board he recognised a man called James Bowen, who had been sentenced to transportation for horse-stealing. Many believe that he guided the ship in the hope of gaining his freedom or to gain vengeance on his employer.

One of the Irish Officers, Lieutenant Barry St Ledger and the Black Legion landed quickly and reached the top of the cliff with forty-seven barrels of gunpowder and twelve boxes of hand grenades. The elderly Colonel Tate, led by James Bowen, came ashore and made Trehowel, home of John Mortimer, his headquarters. Mortimer had employed

Bowen before his incarceration and at this time was preparing for his forthcoming wedding. The French raided his well stocked larder to such an extent that he later received £133 from the Government in compensation. They also raided surrounding farms, slaughtered the poultry, drank wine which the villagers had plundered from a Portuguese coaster wrecked in January and drank any brandy they could lay their hands on. At Brestgarn, a drunken Frenchman fired at a grandfather clock believing that someone was hiding inside. Today the bullet hole can clearly be seen in the case.

Several country folk captured French soldiers, but the heroine of the invasion was Jemima Nicholas, 'a tall, stout, amazon, masculine woman' who worked as a cobbler. She marched from Llanwnda with a pitchfork in her hand and brought back a dozen prisoners, placing them in the guardhouse at Fishguard before returning for more. She lived for 35 years after the invasion, and for her efforts was awarded a government pension of £50 per annum for life. A monument to her heroism can be seen beside the parish church at Fishguard.

News soon reached the Military who were hastily being mobilised to rebuff the Frenchmen. The Pembrokeshire Militia was on duty at Harwich at the time, but the Cardiganshire Militia had taken its place and was on guard at the prison at Pembroke Dock.

On the evening of the 22nd, the Castlemartin Troop had 'conveniently' gathered at Haverfordwest in order to attend the funeral of a comrade. The following morning the Pembroke Fencibles and the Cardiganshire Militia had arrived, together with about fifty Milford Haven seamen. By noon 750 men set out towards Fishguard, under the command of Lord Cawdor.

Colonel Tate who believed that the area was heavily defended decided to seek terms for surrender. Cawdor demanded a complete surrender, and the following morning Tate delivered to him his sword and signed 'articles of capitulation' on a small table which can be seen in the bar of the Royal Oak Inn. His men, except 25 who were too drunk, were assembled on Goodwick Sands where they laid down their arms before being marched from Fishguard to Haverfordwest where they were imprisoned. The last invasion of Britain was over, but many stories remain in the area.

Legend states that when Lord Cawdor saw the women of Fishguard

Carreg Wasted Point — Last Invasion of Britain

Royal Oak Inn at Fishguard

Site of the Tollgate at Efailwen

going about their daily tasks in their red flannel cloaks and tall hats, he ordered them to march up and down the hill, and weave in and out between the trees to give the appearance of a never-ending stream of figures, in full view of the Frenchmen. The men mistook the ladies for the British Grenadier Guards, and decided to surrender. Jemima Nicholas, whom it is believed led the women, became known as the 'General of The Red Army'. Another story tells of two local women, Anne Beach and Eleanor Martin, who brought food to the Frenchmen and helped them to escape in a yacht that belonged to Lord Cawdor himself.

By the 19th century farming was depressed and the population

Grave of Thomas Rees

increasing rapidly. Landowners were forcing small farmers into the hills and, together with high rents, low agricultural prices, and resentment of the poor laws there was much unrest and violence. Life became harder as turnpike roads were improved and rigid collection of tolls made it costly for farmers to take their cattle to market. Poverty led to disease and eventually the situation erupted into riots.

In 1839, the Whitland Trust erected new tollgates on its roads. One of the gates, at Efail-wen, was put into use in time for the lime-carting season. Following a bad harvest this was the last straw for the farmers. Less than one week after the toll-gate was erected, it was set on fire. The gate was re-erected and seven constables employed to protect it but one month later a mob of 400, some disguised as women with black faces, chased the constables away and smashed the gate. On 17 July the gate was destroyed for the third time, by a mob led by 'Becca', who was believed to be the fighter and riot leader Thomas Rees. He was a very large man who had difficulty finding female clothes to fit him, until someone remembered Big Becca, a very large lady who lived in the parish of Llangolman — hence the nickname. From then on the protestors were known as The Rebecca Rioters, or the Daughters of Rebecca, although others say the name derives from the bible — Genesis 24 verse 60. 'And they blessed Rebecca, and said unto her. Thou art our sister, be thou the mother of thousands of millions and let thy seed possess thy gate of those which hate them'. The Rebecca Rioters achieved a notable victory as the Whitland Trust ordered 4 new gates to be dismantled. Meanwhile they continued to reek havoc throughout Pembrokeshire although Thomas Rees took no further part in the riots.

Thomas Rees died suddenly whilst picking a cabbage from his garden for dinner. He was seventy years old and is buried in the graveyard of Bethel Chapel in Mynachlog-ddu. A fitting epitaph on his tombstone when translated reads:

> No one but God know what can happen in a day
> While I was fetching a cabbage for me dinner,
> Death came onto my garden and struck me down.

CHAPTER SEVEN

Some Pembrokeshire Families

No story of Pembrokeshire is complete without a mention of a few of the famous people who lived in the Pembrokeshire area. Giraldus Cambrensis, or Gerald of Wales, is one of the most famous people to have been born and lived in the county.

His father was Sir William de Barri, a Norman knight, whose family took their name from Barry Island off the Glamorganshire coast. His mother was Angharad, the daughter of a Norman lord, Gerald de Windsor, and a Welsh Princess, Nest. Gerald inherited his good looks from this grandmother who, because of her charms, earned herself the name of 'the Welsh Helen of Troy'.

Gerald was born in 1145 at Manorbier Castle and was the youngest of four sons, two older brothers, Robert and Philip, and a half brother Walter. He also had at least one half sister. It is said that from an early age Gerald wanted to become a priest, and as his brothers played and built sand castles and palaces, he built sand churches, which earned him the nickname of 'boy bishop'.

When the Welsh forces attacked nearby Tenby in 1155, Gerald's only concern was to pray in the sanctuary of the church and pleaded to leave the castle.

Whilst Gerald's brothers became loyal Norman Knights, the young priest seems to have concentrated his energies on Welsh ancestry. He studied the history of the church and was often known to quote the legends of Celtic Saints. He was educated at St David's, where his uncle David FitzGerald was Bishop, and then went to St Peter's Abbey at Gloucester before studying at the University of Paris from 1162. On completion of his studies he was appointed Archdeacon of Brecon. When his uncle died in 1176, Gerald was the Chapter's favourite candidate to follow his uncle's footsteps and thus fulfil his great ambition. However, King Henry II appointed the Dutchman Peter de Leia, Prior of Wenlock as Bishop of St David's. Gerald was offered the bishoprics of Bangor and Llandaff, and of Ferns and Leighlin in Ireland but, being bitterly disappointed, refused.

When Peter de Leia died in 1198, Gerald was again the Chapter's favourite but, because he wanted to make St David's a metropolitan see, independent of Canterbury, both the King and the Archbishop of Canterbury opposed his election. On three separate visits to Rome Gerald pleaded his cause before Pope Innocent III without success.

In 1185, at the king's request he accompanied Prince John to Ireland where he was able to meet relatives who, with other Normans, had crossed, in May 1169, from Porthclais to invade Ireland. During his travels he collected material which he used in his books, *'Conquest of Ireland'* and *'Topography of Ireland'*. In 1188 he accompanied Archbishop Baldwin of Canterbury on his tour through Wales to preach the Third Crusade, an interesting and entertaining account of which can be found in Gerald's *Itinerary through Wales*, which was followed by his *Description of Wales*. In 1223, he died and was buried at St David's, the cathedral where he had wished to be Bishop. Had he become bishop, however, the world would have been deprived of a classic contemporary portrait of Wales in the 12th century.

The Wogan family played an important part in the Pembrokeshire life from the thirteenth century, producing no less than 10 sheriffs, two justiciaries of Ireland and a regicide. The Wogans were descended from Gwrgan ap Bleddyn ap Maenarch, Lord of Brecon, but the first Wogan of whom there are any records is his grandson, Sir John. His mother Gwenllian was the daughter of Philip, son of Wizo the Fleming.

Colonel Thomas Wogan of Wiston was one of the judges who sat at the trial of King Charles I and signed the warrant for his execution. His property was sequestered at the Restoration and in 1664 he was arrested and imprisoned in the Tower of London. Colonel Thomas managed to escape and flee to Holland. According to local tradition, disguised, he returned to the neighbourhood of Walwyn's Castle where he changed his

Manorbier castle, home of Gerald of Wales

Carew Castle

name to Drinkwater, and was eventually found dead, a sad and dejected figure in the church porch. The last of the Wiston Wogans, also Thomas, died while taking the waters at the Hotwell springs in Bristol.

Wogans also lived at Picton Castle and the last, John, died in 1420. His daughter and heiress, Katherine, married Owain Dwnn of Kidwelly and they had one son, Henry, who was killed in 1469 on the eve of the battle of Banbury. Picton Castle then passed to his daughter Joan, who married Thomas ap Philip, an ancient Welsh family, and so the name Phillips came to Picton and has remained ever since. One of his descendants, Sir John Phillips, known as 'Good Sir John' became a Member of Parliament in 1700. He was a patron of learning and devoted his time and money to helping the poor. He also organised the building of churches in the London area and founded the Society for the Reform of Manners, which was against swearing and drinking.

Another well known Pembrokeshire man was Sir John Perrot. He was born in 1527 to Mary Berkeley, a royal lady-in-waiting who 'was of the king's familiarity', and the wife of Sir Thomas Perrot of Haroldston, although it is said that King Henry VIII was the true father. Sir Thomas was the son of Sir Owen Perrot, the only Pembrokeshire man ever to be created a Knight of the Holy Sepulchre. John was educated at St David's and entered the household of the Marquis of Winchester, Lord Treasurer of England. Little is known of his life for the next twenty years, although, in 1558 he was granted Carew Castle which had reverted to the crown on Sir Rhys ap Gruffudd's beheading for treason. Sir Thoms built the great Elizabethan block, piped water to the castle, furnished it with Irish rugs, Turkish carpets and stocked the library with books in several languages. In 1562 he was made Vice-Admiral of South Wales, and in the following year became a Member of Parliament for Pembrokeshire. He was three times Mayor of Haverfordwest and became the town's greatest benefactor, leaving property for the benefit of the poor, which to this day is administered by the Perrot's Trustees. In 1566, Queen Elizabeth made him a member of the Commissioners to suppress piracy, although it is said that John made most of his vast fortune by piracy. In 1592 he was accused of treason for criticising his royal half sister, Queen Elizabeth's conduct of foreign policy and accusing her courtiers of being 'effeminate, painted young men with pale faces.' He was placed in the tower, found guilty at

Westminster, sentenced to death, but died of pneumonia at the Tower of London before the sentence could be carried out. Carew Castle once more reverted to the crown. The castle was the scene of a magnificent tournament held in 1507 to celebrate the Knighthood of the Garter bestowed upon Sir Rhys ap Thomas for his support of Henry Tudor at the Battle of Bosworth Field, and by contemporary accounts it was the most splendid entertainment in Welsh history.

We can thank John's father, Sir Thomas Perrot, for the fact that pheasants now occupy Pembrokeshire, for until the end of the sixteenth century none were in the county. According to the historian George Owen, Sir Thomas Perrot, 'procured certain hens and cocks to be transported out of Ireland which he, purposing to endenize in a pleasant grove of his own planting adjoining to his house of Haroldston, gave them liberty therein'. Even today we can see faint traces of a cockpit in a field near the ruined Tudor mansion.

George Owen was born in Henllys in 1552. It is assumed that the house stood above Pont Baldwin where Archbishop Baldwin of Canterbury, with Giraldus Cambrensis, preached the Crusade in 1188. George's father, William Owen, had purchased the lordship of Cemais, and George spent much of his life in litigation over manorial rights, yet he still found time to compile *Description of Pembrokeshire*, which portrays an excellent picture of Pembrokeshire life and customs during the sixteenth century.

Another great Pembrokeshire historian was Richard Fenton, born at Rhosson St David's in 1764, the son of Richard and Martha Fenton. He was educated at the cathedral school before going to Magdalen College Oxford to study law. In 1777 he entered the Middle Temple and in 1783 was called to the bar. Whilst living in London he befriended many notables of the day including David Garrick, Oliver Goldsmith, Samuel Johnson, Edmund Burke, and the painter Joshua Reynolds. David Garrick gave him the freedom of his theatre, and Reynolds painted portraits of Richard and his wife upon ivory miniatures.

One afternoon, while Fenton and Goldsmith were strolling along the lanes of Marylebone they saw a party of young ladies having tea in a garden with an elderly gentleman. When Fenton mentioned that he was struck by the beauty of one of the young ladies Goldsmith took him by the arm and introduced him as 'Mr Fenton, my friend, the celebrated Welsh poet'. They were naturally invited to stay for tea, and Fenton was able to chat to the young lady. On leaving, Fenton asked Goldsmith who their host was. Goldsmith replied 'Never saw him in my life, but I thought if you wanted to flirt with a pretty girl you should!' The infatuated Fenton called several times. The young lady, Eloise, the daughter of the Baron Pillet de Moudon, a Swiss aristocrat who had settled in England as secretary to the Duke of Marlborough, became his wife.

On the death of his uncle Samuel, who died childless, Richard Fenton inherited his uncle's prosperous shipping and fishing business. He was a generous man and when, on account of the Napoleonic wars in 1799, the local people were desperately short of bread, he sent his ships to bring corn from Turkey and Egypt. This he sold at cost to the villagers and free of freight charge.

He settled in Carn-y-garth where he built himself a fine house called Plas Glyn-y-mêl, and planted the garden with exotic trees and shrubs. When he was about to lay the foundation stone, he held a consecration ceremony, and as the vicar was about to complete the service, a woman rushed forward and screamed a curse on him and his children. She maintained that Richard's uncle had promised her a meadow and a cottage at Carn-y-garth in return for her care of him during his old age. Richard immediately made good the promise, and granted her ownership of some land, paying her an annual rental of £30, and providing her, and her daughter, with a comfortable house and garden. Although unaware of his uncle's promise this incident had a profound effect on him. Furthermore, it appears that the woman's curse was fulfilled, as his eldest son, John, quarrelled with him. Richard died in November 1821 and is buried at Manorowen church and left the estate to his next son, who sold it back to John, who in turn squandered it.

General Sir Thomas Picton was born at Hill Street Haverfordwest in 1758, and at the age of thirteen became a standard bearer with the 12th Regiment of Foot, under the command of his uncle, Lieutenant-Colonel William Picton. By 1778, he was promoted to Captain in the Prince of Wales Regiment and was involved in the siege of Gibraltar. When the regiment disbanded, in 1793, Sir Thomas retired to Wales where he remained for the next twelve years, until Britain was at War with France. He then sailed to the West Indies where he commanded a regiment which played a major role in capturing St Lucia in 1796. The following year, after the surrender of Trinidad, he was appointed Military Governor and promoted to Major General. After the siege of Flushing he was appointed its Governor. In 1810, he commanded the Third Division in Portugal and was entrusted by Wellington with the siege of Badajos, where he was wounded and returned to Wales to recuperate. When he had fully recovered, he returned to the Peninsula War in 1813 and chased the French to Toulouse and was awarded the Grand Cross of the Most Honourable Order of The Bath. Once again he retired to his estate at Iscoed, near Ferryside, where he lived with his brother The Reverend Edward Picton.

When Napoleon escaped from Elba, Wellington once again contacted Picton and asked him to join him in the Netherlands. Picton arrived in Brussels on the 15th June, 1815, and while he was at breakfast the following morning he received word that Wellington wished to speak with him. The Duke ordered him to take command of the advance troops, and Picton left immediately for Quatre Bras, where he was hit by a musket ball that fractured his ribs. The next day he progressed to Waterloo, but on the morning of the 18th, although still in great pain from his wound, he led his troops at La Haye Saint where, brandishing his sword, he gave the order to charge. He received a fatal wound to the head, by a musket ball, and died instantly.

Although Picton never married, it is reputed that he had two illegitimate sons, by a woman he met in Trinidad. The boys adopted the mother's Christian name of Rose as their surname, and it is said that one of them came to Haverfordwest in the futile hope of inheriting some of his father's estate.

CHAPTER EIGHT

Life On And Around The Sea

As we have seen in the first chapter, Pembrokeshire grew from the sea, so it is hardly surprising to learn that the coast has always been a great seaway. Because of its unique outline, and the drowned river system at Milford Haven, no part of the county is more than eight miles from the sea. No wonder, then, that Pembrokeshire people have made their living, or gained from the sea, either legally as great sea-faring mariners, or by piracy, smuggling and wrecking.

The old county of Dyfed had a sea-faring tradition long before medieval times, and as we have seen, groups of Mesolithic, Neolithic, Bronze Age and Iron Age people arrived to take up residence, from the south and east in their crude vessels.

In pre-Roman times Pembrokeshire was part of the 'western world' linked by well established sea trading routes. For thousands of years a thriving trade in tools, weapons, items of copper and bronze, gold and iron was carried on from these shores. Some historians believe that there was an old copper mine situated on Ramsey Sound, accounting for the importance of St David's Peninsula as a trading route. At the end of the Roman period the seaways declined, but the Age of the Saints brought a renewed activity when they travelled on their missionary journeys only to be disrupted by the raiding Vikings. However, when the Normans arrived, the area began to develop until, with the colonisation of Normans, Anglo-Saxons and Flemings in south Pembrokeshire 'Little England Beyond Wales' took shape. North Pembrokeshire Welsh continued to resist anglicization.

As the area became more settled, ships became larger and more frequent visitors to the ports, bringing with them cargoes of wines, salt and spices, and exporting wools, hides and a variety of agricultural products. The towns of Pembroke, Tenby and Haverfordwest grew and acquired many wealthy trading merchants. The importance of Haverfordwest can be calculated by the fact that the Mayor was also granted the additional title of 'Admiral of the Port' — a title that exists today.

The area was also the haunt of many pirates who operated along the Pembrokeshire coast. The most notable, during the 16th century, was John Callice, skipper of a ship belonging to Sir John Berkeley, before he took up piracy for a living. Callice was born at Tintern and worked the profitable coves from Lulworth to Pembrokeshire. In January 1577 the Privy Council, aware of Callice's activities, sent a letter to Sir John Perrot, Vice-admiral of Pembrokeshire, asking him to explain how the pirate had managed to slip into Milford, lodge at Haverfordwest and escape out of the county. Sir John made extensive enquiries but was forced to reply that neither he nor the Mayor had any knowledge of the visit.

The seventeenth and eighteenth centuries brought excitement to the Pembrokeshire ports, as a thriving ship building industry grew. By 1800, there were small vessels being built at over thirty coastal sites. The most productive at Cosheston and owned by David Morgan and Thomas Howell. Thirty men and boys were employed at the yard, with the boys serving a seven year apprenticeship. The ships, made from local oak, would take approximately two years to build. They were built mainly for Liverpool ship-owners, and it was customary for the ships' captains to stay at Cosheston during the final stages of the building to supervise and advise on the fitting of rigging and sails. The launch was often performed by the new owner's wife and a dinner, with much drinking, dancing and singing, often into the early hours of the following morning.

Wrecking was a profitable trade too, and Solva, with its entrance of treacherous rocks, made it a haven for the wreckers. It is reputed that the people of Llanunwas Farm were responsible for hanging out false lights to lure the ships into the rocks. Many ships came to grief in the area, not all the work of the wreckers, but nevertheless they were always on hand to collect the spoils. At one time most of the homes in the Solva area had secret cupboards to conceal the smuggled goods from the prying eyes of the authorities.

When the *Oak* was wrecked on the morning of 17th October 1862, it was recorded that the survivors were cared for by the local Lloyds agent at the Cambrian Hotel, whilst the captain John Rees, and James Nash went in search of clothes to replace those stolen by the wreckers.

Another wreck that helped the Pembrokeshire folk was the *Albion* which struck a rock in the 'sound' on April 1837. Fifty passengers were aboard together with a cargo of 180 pigs. The Captain managed to run the Albion onto the beach — since known as Albion Sands — and the pigs swam ashore unaided, where they were met by the villagers of Marloes, who soon converted them into bacon! It was said that the delicious smell of bacon wafted from every house for months.

On another occasion the pillagers received their just deserts for their deeds. In 1791, the merchant vessel *Increase*, carrying a cargo of condemned gunpowder ran ashore at Druidston Haven on her way from a British garrison on the Island of St Kitts. The local people lost no time in arriving on the scene, some to help, others to plunder. They were instructed by the ship's master to unload the personal items, rum and other items on to carts. The barrels of gunpowder were thrown over the side onto the rocks, but some of the villagers thought the copper hoops around the barrels would be useful. Soon the rocks were littered with gunpowder and broken barrels. Meanwhile someone threw a crowbar overboard which hit the rocks and a spark ignited the gunpowder. Eight people were killed instantly and at least 60 women, clad in the fashionable long skirts, were engulfed in the flames and bore the scars for the rest of their lives. This appears to have taught the villagers a lesson because when, on Christmas Day 1810, another ship, *The Linen Hall*, was wrecked at Druidston Haven, there was little plundering, and the ships cargo was actually sold to the locals.

Another ship, the *Phoebe and Peggy*, was wrecked in January 1773 on its journey from Liverpool to Philadelphia. Seven Solva fisherman set out in their boats to rescue the survivors, but as they were returning one of the boats struck Black Rock, and sixty lives were lost. One American lady, Madame Elliot, and her companions had their fingers broken as plunderers stole the gold rings from their fingers. A ballad was written about the wreck of the ship, and one person who heard it was a Liverpool violin maker called Henry Whiteside. At the time he was courting a Solva publican's daughter and was horrified at the events, and decided to change careers, and make a lighthouse. The lighthouse was designed by Henry Whiteside himself, and built using money from a Liverpool dock manager. It was a unique design, an octagonal timber house mounted on six wooden legs, and three cast iron legs. Despite bad weather during construction which Henry braved, the light was lit for the first time on 1st September, 1776.

An interesting story concerns two men who were keeping the lighthouse during a violent storm in the autumn of 1780. One of the men, Joseph Harry died and his colleague, Thomas Griffiths, made a wooden box from some of the interior fittings of the lighthouse, and placed the body inside. Tom had always been known as a bully and was always quarrelling with Joe who was a rather weak man. Fearing that he would be suspected of killing his mate he decided to lash the coffin to a lantern rail, so that he could prove his innocence. Many ships passed and noticed the strange object, but none stopped because the lighthouse was still working. When Thomas Griffiths was relieved of his duties, some 60 days after Joe's death, he was found to be half starved and demented. The remains of Joe were finally laid to rest in the Solva parish churchyard on 26th October, 1780, and Thomas spent the rest of his days in an asylum and died in 1800. Since that day, Trinity House has insisted that all lighthouses must be manned by at least three keepers. The lighthouse was replaced, in 1861, by a modern stone one built under the direction of Sir James Douglas, engineer-in-chief of Trinity House. A reading room was built in the village for the use of the workmen, and there, every Sunday Sir James would conduct a service for the men and their families.

St Brides' Bay was once a thriving herring fishery, and above the beach was once a small chapel where the fishermen prayed for the success of their catch and for a safe return. According to the historian Richard Fenton, stone coffins protruding from the earth in the 17th century were those of the fishermen. The chapel fell into disuse and is reputed to have been converted into a salting house for the fish, but from that day onwards herrings no longer came to St Bride's Bay. Many of the locals will tell you;

When St Bride's chapel a salt house was made,
St Bride's lost the herring trade.

Although acting illegally, smugglers were often aided and abetted by the local customs men and JP's in exchange for the odd bottle or two. There was also a strong contingent of 'respectable Pembrokeshire Admirals' who made a living from a second career. Such as Bartholomew Roberts, Barti Ddu, Black Barti. He was born at Little Newcastle in 1682, the son of a poor farmer, and christened 'John' but assumed the name of Bartholomew. He went to sea from Solva at the age of ten. It is reputed that he never drank anything stronger than tea, which in those days would have cost about £100 a pound, although Barti didn't actually pay for his tea, which was obtained from the East India Company by means of the pistol. He became known as 'the tall sailor with a wholesome laugh', and was a brilliant navigator and an efficient officer although he could rise no further up the ladder. In those days it was who you knew not what you knew, with bribery and corruption being the passport to greater things. He served in the long War of the Spanish Succession and in 1718, he became second mate on the galley *Princess* when it was captured by the *'King James'* captained by the Welsh pirate Hywel Davies. While on board Barti changed sides, and six weeks later when Davies was killed the crew-elected Barti as their captain. From that day on Barti never looked back. After taking rich pickings off the Guinea Coast, he headed for Brazil where he sailed straight into a fleet of forty-two Portuguese men-of-war and took their prize possession, the *Sagrada Familia*, laden with sugar, tobacco and gold. By 1720 his reputation was such that the crew of over twenty ships abandoned them as he entered the harbour at Trepanny in Newfoundland. While anchored here, he captured a French frigate and renamed it appropriately the *Royal Fortune*. The following year he captured another French ship off Guinea and gave this the same name. In just two years he had captured over four hundred treasure ships, with goods and gold which would have been valued at millions of pounds today. In January 1722, off Cape St Lopez, whilst dressed in his 'crimson damask waistcoat and breeches, and red feather in his hat' and eating a breakfast of 'a savoury dish of salmagundi', his luck ran out. *HMS Swallow*, commanded by Captain Chaloner Ogle RN, crept up and fired broadside. Barti was seriously wounded and within a few days he died. He

Stone commemorating Barti Ddu at Little Newcastle

was buried at sea on 5th February 1722, thus ending the life of the most successful pirate of all time. Ogle returned to England, a hero's welcome and a knighthood. But Barti Ddu will always be remembered as the first pirate to fly the skull and crossbones flag. Barti's own invention was black, a skull, grin down and hollow eyed, with an hour glass below with the words: 'Time is Running Out.'

During the American War of Independence, on 15 September 1779 a privateer *Black Prince* appeared off the coast of Fishguard, and a ransom of £500 for a merchant ship, owned by Samuel Fenton, plus a further £500 for the town was demanded by the captain, Stephen Manhant. The Dewsland Volunteers were called to assist but on being refused the ransom the smugglers bombarded the town, hitting several chimneys, and St Mary's Church. Meanwhile, the master of an armed smuggler which was in port returned fire and the *Black Prince* retreated empty handed. The naval adventurer, John Paul Jones, was rumoured to be the culprit, but at the time he was known to be holding the city of Edinburgh to ransom.

Coal played a major role in the success of the Pembrokeshire ports, and has a fascinating history too. The rich seam of anthracite coal on the western end of Pembrokeshire was dug out of bellpits during the medieval period, and is still visible today. The workings had ventilated shafts worked by beam engines with attendant sheds and tramways. In 1324, the Earl of Pembroke received an annual rent of 16s 4d for 'a seam of sea-cole at Coadrath'.

Abel Hicks, who owned the coastal vessels employed in the export trade established the Folkestone Colliery Company in 1769. The small quay and pier built at Nolton Haven have now vanished, but the 'Counting House', still stands overlooking the beach.

Mining of the Pembrokeshire coalfields reached its peak when some thirty or more vessels were being loaded at the same time on Coppet Hall beach. In 1829 a harbour was built at Saundersfoot, several new collieries opened up, and by 1864, over 30,000 tons of coal a year was being exported from Saundersfoot alone. However, the anthracite fields proved difficult to work and shortly after reaching its peak the industry declined and few collieries survived after 1870. The largest, Boville's Court continued to produce coal and in 1926 it reached 35,000 tons in the year. A year later it was closed but re-opened in 1934 and continued production until the outbreak of the second World War.

Another important trade was the shipping of limestone, which was quarried in south Pembrokeshire and exported further afield from the small ports.

The nineteenth century saw the introduction, to Haverfordwest, of the railways and this enabled bulky goods to be transported quicker and cheaper. Consequently the Pembrokeshire sea trade began a slow lingering death such that by 1900 there were few local vessels in operation.

Folk tales concerning mermaids and fishermen were also a part of the Pembrokeshire tradition. An eighteenth century legend tells of a

Typical Pembrokeshire Coracle

fisherman, called Peregrine, who caught a mermaid off Cemmes Head. She told him that if he let her go back to the sea, she would watch over him and call three times if he was in any danger. The fisherman forgot all about the mermaid until one calm day, while fishing, he heard the mermaid call: 'Peregrine, Peregrine, Peregrine, take up your nets, take up your nets'. He was surprised as it was a glorious day, and the sea was like a millpond. However, he obeyed and as he reached the shore a hurricane blew up and he was the only fisherman of twenty to survive.

A curious society of sea serjeants, a Jacobite club, was founded in 1735 in the Pembrokeshire area. The members, drawn from the local gentry, met annually at Tenby and other sea towns in West Wales. They wore a dolphin badge and, from glasses engraved with the dolphin, drank the health of 'The Little Gentleman in Black Velvet'. This was a reference to the molehill on which William III's horse, Sorrel, stumbled in the park at Hampton Court killing the king. As he left no heirs the crown passed to Anne daughter of James II. Why the local gentry were so loyal to James II is not known.

CHAPTER NINE

Some Pembrokeshire Customs

Like every area of Wales, Pembrokeshire is steeped in its own unique set of customs and traditions. It is impossible in this chapter to mention them all, that would take a whole book, but I have outlined a few of the most interesting to give the reader a flavour of the times.

The custom of 'letting-in' the New Year has been traditional in many parts of Britain. In Wales it was marked by the belief that good or bad luck entered the house with the first visitor, according to sex, or personal characteristics. In Pembrokeshire it was considered unlucky for a woman to see a woman, or a man to see a man first. In north Pembrokeshire it was the Christian name that was important. A male named Dafydd (David), Ifan (Evan), Siôn (John) or Siencyn (Jenkin) or a female called Siân (Jane), Sioned (Janet), Mair (Mary) or Margred (Margaret) was considered a lucky omen.

Connected to 'letting in' was the custom of 'New Year Water' which is thought to have dated back to an early pagan ritual to produce rain and, therefore, enhance fertility. At about 3 or 4 am on New Year's morning a group of boys would visit the homes in the neighbourhood carrying a vessel of freshly drawn cold spring water containing a twig of holly, myrtle or some other evergreen. The vessel was normally kept out of sight. The hands and face of every person whom the group met on their rounds would be sprinkled with New Year's water whilst a traditional song was sung. When translated, the song goes:

> Here we bring new water from the well so clear;
> For to worship God with, this happy New Year;

Sing levy dew, sing levy dew, the water and the wine,
With seven bright gold wires and bugles that do whine;
Sing reign of fair maid with gold upon her toe,
Open you the west door and turn the old year go;
Sing reign of fair maid with gold upon her chin.
Open you the east door and let the New Year in.

The giving of gifts on New Year is an ancient custom widely observed in Wales. Like the water custom this began very early in the morning and continued until mid-day. Children carried an apple, studded with oats, raisins and covered in wheaten flour, and topped with a sprig of box or rosemary. In some areas the apple was substituted for an orange. Verses were sung at the door of the house and a gift, sometimes of food, was given to the children. In many remote areas the carrying of an apple has been discontinued although the reciting of verses and greetings still mark the custom. A typical verse sung by Pembrokeshire children, was:

I came today out of my house
with a bag and sticks,
My errand here is to fill
my bag with bread and cheese.

Time has stood still since the 18th century in Cwm Gwaun (*Gwaun Valley*) and, even today, tourists visiting the area around Christmas time, will be forgiven if they are a little confused. In 1582, Pope Gregory XIII ordered that everyone throughout the world should change from the Julian Calender to the new Gregorian Calender, which we use today. In fact this did not take place in Britain until 1752, when September 2nd was immediately followed by the 14th. There was an outcry with people demanding, 'Give us back our eleven days', but the people of the Cwm Gwaun stuck to the old Julian Calender, and celebrate their New Year on the 13th January.

Good Friday also had its fair share of ancient customs. Long reeds were gathered and woven into the form of a man, fixed on a wooden cross and laid in a field or garden. This was known as 'making Christ's bed', and is believed to have originated from an ancient fertility cult observed by the people of Tenby. Another unusual custom was to walk barefoot to church, so as not to disturb the earth.

The first day of May, Calan Mai was, according to the old Celtic

The Wren House from Marloes

The Caseg Fedi

calender, the beginning of summer with the rebirth of all plant life. May Day was a most enjoyable occasion in Pembrokeshire, especially in Tenby. On May Eve, the villagers would place, outside the windows of their homes, boughs of hawthorn in full bloom and decorated with flowers. The thorn blossoms were always used outside as it was considered unlucky to bring them indoors. On May Day itself, the youngsters of the village would dance around the maypoles 'threading the needle'. The poles were decorated with bunches of ribbon and a group of some 30 or more youngsters would wind their way from one pole to another, until they had crossed the town with ribbons.

The last major task of the agriculture year was the gathering of the harvest. Even today the harvest thanksgiving service in church and chapel for a safely gathered crop is well known. But harvest-time was once marked by customs, probably pre-Christian, which with time have lost their significance and become merely an outlet for fun after the hard work.

Men and women helped in the gathering of the harvest and each day's work was rounded off by a supper, which included a dish called *whipod*, consisting of rice, white bread, raisins, currants and treacle. After a meal the party would play games and dance, one called *Dai Siôn Goch*, was danced by two people dressed in ragged clothes and carrying a broom, and probably originated from a fertility rite.

The *caseg fedi*, the harvest *gwrach* (hag), was an object made from the last tuft of corn to be harvested. The head servant would kneel in front of it and divide it into three parts, plaiting them and securing them with straw. The reapers would then stand some distance from the *gwrach* and prepare to throw their reaping hooks at it. Beginning with the head-servant the hooks would be thrown, so that they would travel horizontally just above the ground. Each would take their turn until the sheaf was cut and the successful reaper would call out a verse. When translated it would go something like:

> Early in the morning I got on her track;
>
> Late in the evening I followed her,
>
> I got her, I got her.

The rest of the party would then call out:

> *Beth gest ti?* (What did you get?)

The successful reaper would then shout out, with the rest joining in:
Gwrach, gwrach, gwrach. (A hag, a hag, a hag.)

In some parts of Pembrokeshire, the successful reaper would have the honour of being master for the day. If this happened early in the morning, the rest of the day was spent in games. The most interesting part of the custom was the taking of the *gwrach* into the farmhouse. The householder was warned when the cutting was about to take place, and the women prepared to make the entry difficult. The object was to keep the plaited tuft completely dry and hang it from a beam in the kitchen. The women would fill buckets of water and try to wet the *gwrach*, but as they did not know who the successful reaper was, a great deal of fun was had particularly as the bearer of the sheaf would try to deceive the women, often by concealing the sheaf, under his clothes. If the bearer succeeded in hanging the dry sheaf in its proper place, he was given a place of honour at the supper table and could order as much beer as he wanted.

The major event in any Welsh family home was the wedding of one of its members. A *Gwahoddwr*, or bidder, who was usually a well known local character, would go to friends' and neighbours' homes where he would strike his staff three times on the floor, place his hat under his arm and invite them to the wedding by giving a speech proclaiming the time, date and place of the wedding. At the wedding house gifts were made to the couple. Money would be given or heaved — which means to donate — on the strict understanding that the couple would repay it when the donor, or someone in the donors' family married. The sum donated would be called out and received by the bidder who would enter it into his official ledger — an essential item for a bidding wedding. Many people gave generously, using this as a form of insurance policy against their own wedding, probably one of the earliest forms of hire-purchase agreement, with payments spread over a considerable length of time. As much as £40, a considerable sum of money in the mid 1800s, could be donated in this way and the gifts were considered recoverable by law. To maintain family honour — an important part of Welsh family life — a couple saw to it that the rules were rigidly observed. After the bidding there was the usual wedding feast and entertainments, which consisted of dancing and fiddlers.

Pembrokeshire dealt with unfaithfulness in marriage through an unofficial legal system, whereby each person knew the business and secrets of his neighbour. The name given to this local form of penal custom was *y ceffyl pren* — the wooden horse. When domestic conflict became too much, often because the wife wished to be mistress in her own home, the neighbours would step in to make the man a laughing stock. An effigy of the offender was dressed, and seated on a chair, or wooden horse, and carried on the men's shoulders. The villagers formed a procession preceding and following the effigy, shouting and screaming, and beating saucepans. They halted at intervals, and the chosen spokesman with step forward and describe the offence in verse;

> Ran-dan-dan!
> Betty Morris has beat her man
> What was it with?
> Twas not with a rake, nor yet with a reel
> But twas with a poker, that made him feel.

If the offence was more serious, such as one partner being unfaithful to their marriage vows, the villages would seize the offending persons and tie them back to back on the wooden horse. The faithless couple would then be paraded through the streets of the village, where they would be pelted with rotten fruit and eggs.

Christmas in Wales was once an important festival. In north Pembrokeshire Christmas Day marked the beginning of *Y Gwyliau* — a three week holiday when farming was suspended. The plough was carefully carried into the home and placed under the table in the kitchen. On Christmas Day itself all the farmers and cottagers in the area were invited to the largest farm to share in a meal of goose, beef and pudding. As the holiday progressed the men went from house to house and were invited into the *rwm ford* — the room where the meals were eaten. As they sat around the table drinking beer, which had been kept warm in a brass pan, they would wet the idle plough with their beer to symbolise that it had not been forgotten.

Another ancient custom, called the Mari Lwyd or *Grey Mare*, is no longer followed but is believed to have survived from the Middle Ages mystery plays. A man would wear a horse skull, bedecked with ribbons, and, accompanied by a group of singers, would be serenaded from house to house. A variation of this could be seen at Tenby where a man would

A Reaping Party

Mari Lwyd

dress up as 'The Lord Mayor of Penniless Cove'. He wore a mask and flowers or ribbons and was carried in a chair by attendants with flags and violins. He blessed each house and gave the party something for Christmas.

An interesting custom, that has puzzled ethnologists, is the carrying of a wren in a 'wren-house' from house to house on Twelfth Night. Local variations of the custom are known throughout Wales, but an early Pembrokeshire version is given by Edward Lhuyd (1660-1709) published in his *Parachialia*, and translated in 1910 by Dr I. G. Peate in *Archaeologica Cambrensis:*

> "They are accustomed in Pembrokeshire etc to carry a wren in a bier on Twelfth Night; from a young man to his sweetheart, that is two or three bear it in a bier (covered) with ribbons, and sing carols. They also go to other houses where there are no sweethearts and there will be beer etc. And a bier from the country they call *Cutty Wran* — Little Wren."

This custom was still being performed in the nineteenth century, and a collection at the Welsh Folk Museum includes a wren house from Marloes, made in 1869. Like the 'bier' described by Lhuyd it is decorated with ribbons and was carried in procession on Twelfth Night, the wren having been caught and imprisoned beforehand. As the procession made its way to each house it sang the following song:-

> Joy, health, love and peace; we're here in this place;
> By your leave here we sing concerning our King.
> Our King is well drest in silks of the best
> And the ribbons so rare, no King can compare,
> Over hedges and stiles we have travelled many miles,
> We were four foot-men in taking this wren.
> We were four at watch and were nigh of a match
> Now Christmas is past, Twelfth Day is at last.
> To the old year adieu, great joy to the new.
> Please turn the King in.

In Tenby the version is slightly different. Having acquired the wren, it was placed in a small ornamented box, or paper house, with a square of glass at either end. Two or four men would carry the container, elevated on four poles fixed to the corners, and enter the house, groaning under the weight of their burden.

The version used around 1890, in the Solva district, again differs slightly as the house may be substituted by a lantern decked with ribbons and a sparrow used in place of a wren.

There are many ceremonies associated with death in Wales, and Pembrokeshire is no exception. One strange custom recorded in the middle of the eighteenth century was to draw the corpse through the chimney of the house before placing it in the coffin.

An unruly game called knappen, possibly a forerunner to rugby football, but without boundaries, was started at St Meugan in Cemais, near Llanfair Nantgwynwas. It was played by an unlimited number of men, parish against parish, who wore a light pair of breeches and were stripped to the waist. The game began with the tossing between teams of a knappen — a wooden ball of yew, box, crab or holly that had been boiled in oil to make it slippery. The object was to carry the ball as far as possible into one's own parish, and play would often not cease until nightfall. Footmen were permitted to use their fists, and mounted players allowed to carry a club with which they were allowed to strike players who refused to give up the ball when challenged. George Owen of Henllys, writing in 1600 complained that the rules were little observed, with the footmen working out private grudges. It is reputed that George Owen suffered badly while playing the game in the later part of the sixteenth century and carried the scars of his injuries for the rest of his life. A major event with some two thousand men took place on Corpus Christi between Cemais and Emlyn, in nearby Cardiganshire. Many stalls provided food and drink for the many spectators who came to cheer their team.

CHAPTER TEN

The Growth of Pembrokeshire to Modern Times

Pembrokeshire always has been a thriving county and, the 'Milford Mail Coach' one of the fastest forms of transport in the county, covered the 356 miles from London in 'just' 36 hours. Naturally the Milford Mail was in demand as it connected with the packet boats, which sailed from Milford Haven to Waterford in Ireland. However, the county really began to develop when Isambard Kingdom Brunel decided to bring to it his Great Western Railway.

On 28th December, 1853, Haverfordwest was decorated with banners and bunting and the residents lined the streets to welcome the arrival of the first train, built by the South Wales Railway at Cartlett. Little did the people know that this happy day was to mark the beginning of the decline of Haverfordwest as port.

But the coming of the railways was foretold in the late eighteenth century by Thomas Evan's wife Sarah, some fifty years before George Stephenson first introduced the steam locomotive. They lived on a small farm named Penyfeidr, near Trefgarn Rocks and Sarah was known for her ability to see into the future. One day she returned home and said she had just witnessed a wonderful sight in Trefgarn Valley below her house. She described a large number of heavily laden carts travelling very fast one after the other. There was no horse or bullock to pull them, but the first wagon seemed to be on fire as smoke was ascending into the sky from it.

When Brunel first brought the railway to Pembrokeshire, he intended to extend it northwards towards Fishguard cutting through the Trefgarn

Valley, and thus fulfil Sarah's prophecy. However, he abandoned the scheme, and instead, built the line to New Milford, now Neyland. Later a branch line was opened a few miles to the north of Trefgarn and eventually, on discovering that the line via Letterson, was unsuitable for a fast direct line to London, GWR constructed a new line from Goodwick through the Trefgarn Valley, just below Sarah's house. Thus Brunel's original idea and Sarah's prophecy were fulfilled and the line remains in use today.

Milford Haven was planned and developed during the 1790s by Charles Francis Grenville. He was helped by a Frenchman, Jean Louis Barrallier, and an American, Benjamin Rotch. They obtained the help of a colony of Quaker whale fishermen from Dartmouth, Nova Scotia, who wanted to find a better headquarters for storing their sperm oil, which at the time was used for lighting London streets. The town was built on the east bank of an inlet on the north shore of the drowned valley of the Haven and it's streets laid out in the American system of parallel lines.

Shipbuilding continued under private ownership, but commercial activities remained at a low level, until the docks were built between 1874 and 1888 to capture the transatlantic trade from Liverpool and Southampton. The first vessel to enter Milford Haven was the steam trawler *Sybil* on 27 September 1888 but the transatlantic trade was never captured.

In the early 1950's Milford Haven was rediscovered as a port when BP and Esso were looking to develop an oil port to enable them to keep pace with the rising demand for petroleum products. They were planning to use oil tankers of 100,000 cwt or more and, with cheap plentiful land and a silt-free waterway Milford Haven was highly suitable. Government approval was given and by 1959, both Esso and BP had embarked on major building programmes.

The first oil refinery was built by Esso near the village of Herbrandston and was fully operational by the autumn of 1960. Today it is the second largest refinery in the British Isles.

By 1961, BP's refinery at Popton Point near Angle, was fully operational. However, it was decided to build the deep water terminal at the existing refinery at Llandarcy, near Swansea. Crude oil is imported here and transported the 60 miles to Milford through an impressive

Milford Haven Heritage and Maritime Museum

Refinery Railway stock at Milford Haven Docks

network of pipelines which cross twelve major roads, and no less than thirty-seven rivers.

Since Esso and BP came to Milford Haven, the town continues to thrive through Texaco, Gulf Oil and Amoco all bringing their operations to the area.

Pembroke Dock, a mile north of the old town of Pembroke, came into existence when the Admiralty transferred the naval dockyard from Milford in 1814. For over 112 years the dockyard prospered with over 260 ships being built — the first steam man-of-war *HMS Tartar*, the first propeller driven warship, *HMS Conflict*, and the first of several royal yachts — *The Victoria* and *Albert* in 1843.

HMS Windsor Castle was launched on 14 September 1852, but when it became known that the Duke of Wellington had died that day, the name was changed in his honour. The *HMS Duke of Wellington* became the flagship of Admiral Napier during the Crimean War and led the grand review of the Fleet by Queen Victoria in 1855. The last ship built at Pembroke, the *Oleander*, was launched in 1922 and four years later the dockyard was closed, bringing vast unemployment to the area.

In 1930, the Royal Air Force established a base at Pembroke Dock, home to the famous Sunderland flying-boats during World War II, and remained here until the 1960's. During the war the area was a favourite target of the Luftwaffe and, in August 1940, the oil storage tanks at Llanreath were bombed, starting one of the most serious fires seen in Britain.

In more recent times Pembroke Dock has seen the starting up, in 1979, of a ferry service to Cork, and in the following year to Rosslare. By the end of the eighties the old Royal Dockyard was developed into a deep water port and the town now is part of the enterprise zone of Wales.

Most holiday makers, however, come to Pembrokeshire to walk along the Coastal Path and enjoy the natural beauty of the rugged coastline. It is also a naturalist's paradise. The Pembrokeshire Coastal Path, one of the finest in Britain, was first explored, in 1951, by R. M. Lockley, a Pembrokeshire naturalist. As tourism grew, the Government decided in February 1952 to designate the coastline as a National Park. The Pembrokeshire Coastal Path was eventually opened on 16 May 1970, by the broadcaster and traveller Wynford Vaughan Thomas, and keeps as close to the cliff edge and the seashore as safety allows. There are a few diversions of course, around Milford, Tenby and Fishguard, and the army still has a firing range at Linney Head, prohibiting access at certain times. The path's attractiveness varies with the seasons, the early part of the summer seeing the sea birds at the height of their breeding activities with colonies of guillemots and razor bills all fighting for an inch of space on the narrow cliff borders. The path is well signposted and its official length is 167 miles, 269km.

The islands around the coast of Pembrokeshire are alive with many exotic birds. Skomer, originally 'Scalmy' — The Island of the Sword — in the days of the Vikings, is now a National Nature Reserve managed by Dyfed Wildlife Trust. The Trust is now in the process of installing viewing facilities so we can share the lives of the gulls, gannets, razorbills, guillemots, terns and puffins. The island is also the home of the unique Skomer vole.

Skokholm was the first observatory to be established in Britain and Grassholm has the largest gannet colonies in the world. Next to Scotland, Pembrokeshire can boast the largest population of Atlantic grey seals. They breed on Ramsey and Skomer islands and under the mainland cliff, producing some 400 pups per year. It is also famous for its Manx shearwaters and storm petrels.

Grassholm is situated some 15 miles out into the Atlantic and has a vast colony of gannets. In the *Mabinogi* this was the isle of Gwales, where the mythical King Brân's severed head was brought by his grieving followers after he was fatally wounded in battle in Ireland.

Pembrokeshire is still thriving and with the completion of the M4 and the A48/A40 trunk roads to St Clears, the county is becoming accessible to more people.

In the spring of 1992, the Landsker Trail linked circular routes to create long distance walks around the entire Landsker Borderlands, for all to enjoy.

The 'Milford 2000 Plan', is a scheme launched in 1990 by Milford Haven Port Authority, in partnership with the Government to encourage and breathe new life into Milford Docks with such attractions as the Milford Haven Heritage and Maritime Museum, the Docklands Gallery and a new Fish Market. During mid 1992, the first Industrial Park units were occupied, bringing a mixture of tourism, leisure and light industry to the county, promising an ever expanding prosperous future for the county.

Why not come and see and explore this corner of Wales for yourself? You won't be disappointed.

Selected Bibliography

Williams, Gwyn, *The Land Remembers — A View of Wales*. (Faber and Faber 1977)

Lloyd, J. E., *A History of Wales* (Ernest Benn 1930)

Walker, David, *Medieval Wales* (Cambridge University Press 1990)

Jones, T. Gwynn, *Welsh Folklore and Folk Custom* (Pub 1930)

Lockley, R. M., *Pembrokeshire* (Robert Hale 1957)

Sticklings, Thomas G., *The Story of Saundersfoot* (H. G. Walters 1970)

Fenton, Richard, *Historical Tour Through Pembrokeshire* (Brecknock 1903)

Trevor Herbert and Gareth Elwyn Jones, *Tudor Wales* (University Press of Wales Cardiff 1988)

Lewis Thorpe, *Gerald of Wales — The Journey Through Wales/The Description of Wales (Penguin Classics 1978)*

Acknowledgements

All illustrations copyright of C. Hughes
except
cover photograph
(by kindness of the National Trust)

The Wren House, The Caseg Fedi, A Reaping Parti,
Mari Lwyd
(Welsh Folk Museum)

The Story of Gower

by Wendy Hughes

incl. map, many illustrations, 87 pages,

Wendy Hughes' "The Story of Gower" takes the reader from the cave dwellers icy existence to modern day Gower, drawing on a richly woven pageant of history, legends and notorious characters, that will hold the readers attention until the last page is turned.